#28504832

# FIELD GUIDE TO STRATEGY

HARVARD BUSINESS / THE ECONOMIST REFERENCE SERIES

**Field Guide to Business Terms:** *A Glossary of Essential Tools and Concepts for Today's Manager*

**Field Guide to Marketing:** *A Glossary of Essential Tools and Concepts for Today's Manager*

**Field Guide to Strategy:** *A Glossary of Essential Tools and Concepts for Today's Manager*

# FIELD GUIDE TO STRATEGY:

*A Glossary of Essential Tools
and Concepts
for Today's Manager*

CHIEF CONTRIBUTOR
## Tim Hindle

EDITED, WITH AN INTRODUCTION BY
## Margaret Lawrence

*Boston, Massachusetts*

Published in the United States by Harvard Business School Press

Printed in the United States of America

98  97  96  95  94        5  4  3  2  1  (pb)

98  97  96  95  94        5  4  3  2  1  (hard)

*Field Guide to Strategy* is part of the Harvard Business/The Economist Reference Book Series and is based on material first published in Great Britain in 1993 by The Economist Books Ltd.

The paper used in this publication meets the requirements of the American National Standard for Permanence of Paper for Printed Library Materials Z39.49-1984.

Library of Congress Cataloging-in-Publication Data

Hindle, Tim.
    Field guide to strategy : a glossary of essential tools and concepts for today's manager / chief contributor Tim Hindle ; edited, with an introduction by Margaret Lawrence.
        p.   cm. — (Harvard Business/The Economist reference series)
    ISBN 0-87584-436-7 (hard : alk. paper) — ISBN 0-87584-431-6 (pbk. : alk. paper)
    1. Strategic planning — Terminology.   I. Lawrence, Margaret, 1950–.   II. Title.   III. Series: Harvard Business/The Economist reference series.
    HD30.28.H553   1994
    658.4'012—dc20                                      93-26047
                                                        CIP

Series design by Mike Fender

# CONTENTS

# FIELD GUIDE TO STRATEGY

# INTRODUCTION

*Field Guide to Strategy* is one of a series of books designed to interpret the vocabulary that has resulted from the professionalization of management in the last two decades and to make it accessible to even the occasional user. It is written by Tim Hindle, a former management editor of *The Economist,* and edited by Margaret Lawrence, the former North American editor for Strategic Directions Publishers.

In the complex and fluid organizations characteristic of the best-managed companies of the 1990s, managers are frequently asked to step out of familiar territory, perhaps as members of teams or task forces or on call as functional specialists. Even more to the point, in today's boundaryless organization there is considerable overlap in responsibilities, and functional specialties may be disappearing altogether.

Because of its general importance to business success, every manager (or would-be manager) wants to be at home in the heady realm of strategy. A significant body of writing and research has generated an array of concepts and terms designed to "enhance" our understanding of the topic. At the same time, a broader group of people has assumed responsibility for strategy. No longer the product of a specialized corporate staff, strategy development and implementation now belongs to line management (nonspecialists). Further, in an effort to build commitment, executives have increased their communications about strategy; the result is a wide range of employees exposed to top-level strategic thinking.

In short, more people are involved, at least peripherally, in some aspect of the development or implementation of strategy. Perhaps it is a line manager preparing a plan for a new product, an entrepreneur involved in an acquisition, or a professional or technical employee seeking a better understanding of where the organization is going. Readers are likely to encounter strategy-related terms in meetings, in communications from top management, and in the general business press. They may even need to use them to communicate their own ideas effectively to management.

Following an essay on the evolution and current state of the art in the field of strategy is a glossary of definitions of terms related to strategy. We have tried to include only definitions that relate directly to strategy and are most likely to be used in a discussion about strategy. For terms in more general use, we have chosen definitions that address their meaning in the business environment. Since our brief discussions of very complex terms cannot be comprehensive, we have included thought-provoking entries connected to one or two major aspects of the definition, always from the perspective of what the nonspecialist might need to know. Throughout we have scattered quotations that we hope will bring the terms to life. In the glossary, related entries are connected through cross-references; words in capitals usually indicate a separate entry, thus enabling readers to find other relevant information (although they should note that abbreviations and acronyms are also in capitals).

We have elected to include material on individual companies that have pioneered or are otherwise exemplary of the application of the concepts defined here; these entries are only illustrative. The companies are well known and are often referred to in discussions about strategy, and their descriptions, like the definitions of the glossary terms, are not meant to be exhaustive. Readers are invited to pursue additional information about the companies profiled in *Field Guide to Strategy* as examples of strategic thinking applied to the real world of business.

# PART 1

# *STRATEGY IN CONTEXT*

# STRATEGY IN CONTEXT

The word "strategy" comes from the Greek *strategia*, meaning "generalship." Of military origin, strategy is the art or science of planning a war, and much of the original management thinking on strategy treated business as something of a war, with the CEO as the general, or chief architect, of strategy, backed up by well-drilled and obedient ranks of corporate soldiers. Indeed, learned commentary on strategy nearly always includes a pithy quote or two from General Von Clausewitz, or Sun Tzu. Less bellicose commentators tend to draw sports analogies, usually football but occasionally horse racing. Although the context differs, the message is much the same: "We're in this to win."

However, times have changed. CEOs are no longer generals, workers are not soldiers. In everyday parlance, strategy is a plan for getting something done. It includes both a vision of what needs to be done and a plan for how to do it. It doesn't necessarily imply winning (if what you mean by winning is that the competition loses), just achieving your goals — more on this later.

## STRATEGY DEFINED

Although the term "strategy" has been around for centuries, only within the past 30 years has it been applied to business and evolved as a management discipline. The entry of strategy into the lexicon of business reflected both the increasing complexity of the corporation and its environment and the professionalization of management. Leaders of the one-product/single-market companies characteristic of most business until after World War II didn't have to think much about strategy: choices were simple and decisions tended to be obvious. As companies grew, they broadened their product lines and entered a wider variety of markets. At the same time they encountered more competitors, added more employees (layers of management), and acquired more stakeholders. With more choices, the question of what to do and how to get it done became more complex. Management needed both the concepts and the vocabulary to address the problem.

The first authors to write about the concept of strategy in a management context were Alfred Chandler, Kenneth Andrews, C. Roland Christensen, and Igor Ansoff, all in the mid-1960s. Chandler defined strategy as ". . . the determination of the basic long-term goals and objectives of an enterprise, and the adoption of courses of action and the allocation of resources necessary for carrying out these goals." (Alfred D. Chandler, Jr., *Strategy and Structure: Chapters in the History of American Industrial Enterprise* [Cambridge, Mass., MIT Press, 1962].) Andrews and Christensen believed that strategy was the unifying theme that linked together the separate functional areas in a company and related its activities to its external environment. Their fundamental premise was that a company's strengths and weaknesses should be applied to dealing with opportunities and threats presented by its environment. The challenge to management, given both a set of opportunities and a set of resources, was to realize a relative competitive advantage — to win and to make a profit as a result. Ansoff identified the four main components of strategy: a product/market scope, a growth vector (a planned change in the product/market scope), competitive advantage (those specific attributes of individual product/ markets that gave the firm a strong competitive position), and synergy (a measure of joint effects; the 2 + 2 = 5 phenomenon).

These authors were writing at a time when finance, production, and marketing were being developed as management disciplines, when there was a dangerous tendency to think of an organization as the sum of its individual functional areas. These authors provided a holistic view of the corporation in the face of an increasing emphasis on the corporation as a collection of individual functions. Their work brought strategy to the forefront of management thinking, and it has been there ever since. Although much has been written subsequently about strategy, the original work remains valid and relevant today.

## A BRIEF HISTORICAL OVERVIEW

Subsequent management literature was filled with discussions of strategy, elaborating on aspects of the problem outlined by Andrews and Ansoff. Next came a period of fascination with articulating the "right" strategy. Analytical techniques, using the "right" tools and following the right sequence of steps, were devised to find it. Strategic planning was born. Not only an academic discipline, but also an industry, management strategy consulting evolved to help companies find the right strategy.

The search for sources of competitive advantage became increasingly complex. In the 1960s and 1970s, rapidly diversifying companies participated in so many different markets and had at their disposal so many analytical tools and concepts that strategic planning became a full-time staff function. Soon corporate strategy was distinguished from business strategy; portfolio management techniques were developed to govern the all-important resource allocation process in large corporations. Corporate strategy wasn't limited to existing businesses. In the 1970s, with the help of portfolio management techniques, corporations eagerly acquired unrelated but "attractive" businesses. This acquisition spree, fueled by a hyperactive stock market, required even more analysis — more tools and more staff.

The ultimate refinement of analytical approaches to strategy is undoubtedly the work of Michael Porter. Building on Ken Andrews' exhortation to "examine the economic environment of the company to determine the essential characteristics of the industry, to note its developments and trends," Porter provided a systematic approach to assessing a firm's competitive environment. He transferred principles developed in the field of microeconomics on the structural determinants of industry profitability into a strategic context. His research has shown how a system of forces from inside and outside an industry collectively influence the nature and degree of competition within it and, ultimately, its profit potential. The strategic implication of Porter's work was the conclusion that a firm should position itself within the industry to maximize competitive advantage. Competitive advantage can arise either from lower cost or from the ability to differentiate the product or service to command a premium price and is the result of discreet activities a firm performs in creating, producing, marketing, and delivering the product or service. These activities compose the value chain. After Porter, simple conceptual approaches no longer seemed adequate. Interestingly, although Porter reduced all strategies to one of two — compete on cost or differentiate — his comprehensive framework for analysis was the fulfillment of the threats/opportunities versus strengths/weaknesses framework established by his mentors, Andrews and Christensen.

The tools and analytical techniques developed in the mid-1970s gave executives a good idea of what they should be doing. Finding the right strategy became easier. Having the right strategy, however, didn't necessarily lead to success in the marketplace. Certain problems emerged. Concepts such as the experience curve and the growth/share matrix proved to have limitations. Elegant enough in their simplicity, they proved simplistic when translated from theory into practice. Conglomerates discovered that they couldn't run their unrelated businesses, and investors realized that they could diversify their own portfolios. Most acquisitions failed, and were eventually divested, often at a loss. Executives learned that elegant strategies developed by their own planning staffs or by outside consultants lacked credibility with line management whose support was crucial to successful implementation.

Critics tended to dismiss the concepts and trends that once ruled the day in the field of strategy as fads or fashions and applauded companies for "getting back to basics," as if management had suddenly returned to its senses. In truth, strategy, as a relatively young discipline, went through a stage of rapid growth. The original tools and analytical techniques of strategy had staying power and provided the field with a frame of reference, a common vocabulary. The discipline may have become more sophisticated, but many of these concepts, a good number of which are included in the Glossary, are still useful.

However, managers have discovered that no science, no theory, no formula can tell them how to run their businesses. The reason — theory will always differ from reality. Analytical techniques assume a static reality and cannot be translated easily to the dynamic world of business. There is a complex and ongoing relationship between the firm and its environment. Because the corporate context is in constant flux, the threats, the opportunities, the objectives, and the focus of strategy change over time. Furthermore, strategy doesn't just happen; it takes people and commitment, the so-called human side of strategy, to develop and implement it. It is now apparent that this side of strategy is as important as elegant analysis to the actual achievement of competitive advantage.

## TODAY'S REALITIES

*Simplicity . . . Too often we measure everything and understand nothing. The most important things you need to measure in a business are customer satisfaction and cash flow. If you're growing customer satisfaction, your global market share is sure to grow too. Employee satisfaction gets you productivity, quality, pride and creativity. And cash flow is the pulse — the key vital sign of a company.*

Jack Welch, General Electric

Noel M. Tichy and Stratford Sherman, *Control Your Destiny or Someone Else Will: How Jack Welch Is Making General Electric the World's Most Competitive Company* (Doubleday/Currency, 1993)

The corporate strategic planning staffs are mostly gone now. In fact, today's leaner organization is likely to have eliminated layers of management and trimmed headquarters count. Strategy has become the responsibility of line management — and, to an extent, the responsibility of every worker. There is less emphasis on analysis, more emphasis on implementation, and a greater realization that successful implementation requires both vision and commitment. A "back to basics" movement in strategy began when consultants Tom Peters and Bob Waterman, in their book *In Search of Excellence*, revealed that the best-managed companies "stuck to their knitting" (that is, avoided the diversification excesses of the mid-1970s). Later academics C. K. Prahalad and Gary Hamel stressed "core competencies" as the unifying thread in successful diversified companies and "strategic intent" as the sense of shared vision that drives successful implementation and competitive success.

These important trends reflect significant changes in the business environment.

## THE CUSTOMER IS BACK

One of the oldest adages in business is "the customer is always right." In today's successful corporation, the customer reigns supreme. At some point business forgot (at least in the United States) that the customer wanted quality. The relentless pursuit of market share through aggressive cost cutting inspired by experience curve-based strategies assumed that price was all that mattered to the customer. The Japanese didn't share this vision, and the rest is history. Today's customer demands quality and value. Today's organization is realigning itself so that all elements serve the customer. This is accompanied by a drive to improve quality and productivity, also inspired by Japanese practices.

## YOU CAN WIN BY COOPERATING

Yesterday's organization was at war with everyone. Adversarial relationships with suppliers were believed to result in the best price and service. Customers' demands were viewed with suspicion. Today's managers are discovering the value of cooperation. Strategic alliances with noncompetitors are formed to spread the cost of market development, speed technology transfer, and so forth. Suppliers become partners through long-term supply contracts and shared information systems and are encouraged to contribute to product and process improvements. Consortia pursue precompetitive research.

## GLOBALIZATION

As consumer tastes and lifestyles around the world become more similar, global strategies are taking shape. With the help of sophisticated information systems, corporations can realistically expect to control and coordinate activities around the world in a meaningful sense. Global strategies involve not only selling worldwide, but also producing and even conducting research in more than one location. In global strategy the firm can choose to locate the various activities in its value chain anywhere. It must choose how to configure these activities worldwide to maximize competitive advantage. Equally important, the corporation, no matter how limited its market, must prepare to encounter global competitors.

### INFORMATION TECHNOLOGY IS REDEFINING THE ORGANIZATION

At last cost-effective and user-friendly information technology is making information-based strategies possible. Shared access to information speeds response time, reduces cost, and in the long run improves decision making. Corporations use technology to link up with both suppliers and customers through "channel partnerships"; they are reengineering business processes to eliminate routine activities such as preparing invoices as well as many steps in the order-processing cycle. Shared information systems are the enabling factor behind other significant changes such as leaner, less hierarchical organizational structures and employee empowerment.

### HUMAN RESOURCES HAS GAINED STRATEGIC IMPORTANCE

Access to information has empowered employees to make decisions, and corporations are finally realizing that employees are in a position to offer some pretty good suggestions. This has the additional benefit of enabling the organization to eliminate steps in the corporate hierarchy formerly devoted primarily to supervision and information processing. Simplified decision-making processes have cut costs and increased the speed of decision making, which is especially critical in today's rapidly changing environment. People are becoming the critical aspect of competitive advantage, and this has led to an increased emphasis on education and the management of diversity to bring out the best in employees.

## CHANGE MANAGEMENT

Static solutions no longer suffice because the pace of change has intensified. Technology has shortened product life cycles, competitors move more swiftly, and markets are more fluid. Competitive advantage goes to the swiftest, so companies have organized to make rapid response a competitive weapon. In addition, management has begun to take active steps to help employees deal with the tension and ambiguity that constant change brings.

## VALUES

When discussing the massive changes that his company, General Electric, has experienced since he became CEO in 1981, Jack Welch stressed the importance of values:

> *Every organization needs values, but a lean organization needs them even more. When you strip away the support system of staffs and layers, people need to change their habits and expectations or else the stress will just overwhelm them. We're all working harder and faster. But unless we're also having more fun, the transformation doesn't work. Values are what enable people to guide themselves through that kind of change.*

**PART 2**

# *GLOSSARY*

## Acquisition management

A decisive, often dramatic strategic move, the acquisition is very tempting. No matter what its potential, however, realizing the benefits of an acquisition is a difficult task: too many acquisitions are done in haste and regretted at leisure. Philippe C. Haspeslagh and David B. Jemison in *Managing Acquisitions: Creating Value through Strategic Renewal* (Free Press, 1991), assert that the key to realizing the benefits of an acquisition is the integration of the acquired firm. This process requires seven concurrent management initiatives:

- Establishment of a formal interface management and gatekeeping structure
- Creation of careful communication to employees, customers, and suppliers to keep everyone operating on an even keel
- Creation of a new sense of purpose to motivate acquired employees
- Consolidation of control by the acquirer by continuing to seek out and verify information gathered in the premerger phase
- Reduction of resistance to change in the acquired organization by the acquirer
- Development of mutual understanding vital to transfer of capabilities within the merged organization
- Enhancement of management credibility in the acquiring firm by producing early results, and in the acquired firm by truthful communications, fairness, and an ability to deliver on resource commitments

## ACTIVITY-BASED COSTING

An alternative to traditional cost accounting systems that allocate indirect costs on the basis of direct labor or machine hours, activity-based costing (ABC) assigns direct costs and support expenses by activity, and assigns these expenses to the drivers of the activity. For a product cost analysis, ABC divides costs into a hierarchy of activities that include unit-level activities (direct expenses), batch-level activities (including machine setup time and material movements), product-sustaining activities (such as process engineering and product specifications), and facility-sustaining activities (plant management, heat, building and grounds). The important point is that not all costs vary directly with volume; some products make heavy demands on support resources.

Similarly, some large customers may be less profitable than others because they require technical support, or order small quantities of a wide variety of products. ABC analysis, according to Robin Cooper and Robert S. Kaplan of Harvard Business School, leads to two types of actions:

1. Raising prices on products that make heavy demands on support prices and lowering prices on high-volume products that do not.
2. Taking action to reduce resource consumption. This may mean changing the product mix or implementing programs for CONTINUOUS IMPROVEMENT.

## AGENTS AND PRINCIPALS

An agent is a person authorized by a principal to act on his or her behalf. Part of an agent's responsibility is to try to act at all times in the best interests of the principal.

Put that into the context of the relationship between the managers of a company and its owners (i.e., shareholders), and you have what is known as the "agency problem." In olden times, managers were true agents of an individual landlord or merchant; every so often they were expected to account for their stewardship through an audit (or hearing).

Nowadays managers are employees of huge public companies. It is not possible for them to have the relationship of agent to principal that the eighteenth-century manager had with a sole proprietor. As a group, shareholders are far too nebulous for that to be possible.

Today's manager has wider responsibilities (to employees, to the environment, to government) that are often in conflict with his or her responsibility to shareholders. And as responsibility filters down the management ladder, the other responsibilities intrude more and more into the agency relationship.

The agency problem exists because the principal can neither monitor the agent's actions perfectly nor have access to perfect information. The agent almost always has more information than the principal has, and the agent's incentives and perspective usually differ from those of the principal. Symptoms of the agency problem include insider trading scandals, golden parachutes, and a dramatic increase in executive compensation in the United States.

### ALLIANCE

In some aspects of strategy, cooperation is more effective than competition. Increased research and development costs, the increasing complexity of technology, the blending of technologies, the increased use of complex technology in a broad range of products (e.g., microprocessors in television sets), and the need to move quickly in rapidly evolving markets are just some of the factors behind a growing interest in alliances.

Alliances are cheaper than internal development and often necessary for access to proprietary technology. Forms of alliances include JOINT VENTURES, CONSORTIA, license agreements, CHANNEL PARTNERSHIPS, cross-marketing agreements, and long-term supply contracts.

Management issues related to alliances include the following:

- Anxiety about loss of control over part of the business
- Fear of becoming too dependent on an outside organization
- Fear of leakage of proprietary/confidential information to a potential competitor
- Potential resistance from parts of the organization that may be threatened by the alliance
- The difficulty of working closely with an organization that has a different culture

The following are keys to a successful alliance:

- Senior-level commitment
- Clear identification and active management of likely risks and sources of conflict
- A clear understanding by each partner of the alliance's objectives
- Agreement between the partners on goals, objectives, and desired outcomes
- Explicit quantitative and qualitative measures of success

## AMERICAN EXPRESS

The most powerful market-driven group in the world, American Express built its preeminence on two intangible assets:

- The double signature as a security device on its travelers' checks, which celebrated their centenary in 1991. In their first century, over 10 billion American Express travelers' checks were issued; although this represents only a small proportion of the company's revenues, the operation continues to be highly profitable.

- The strong consumer franchise that surrounds American Express' charge card operations and allied services.

Like many companies during the 1980s, however, American Express became a holding company. Its New York headquarters presided over a collection of independent business units operating in diverse financial services arenas; these included the brokerage house Shearson Lehman. In the 1990s, American Express was persuaded by circumstances — particularly the loss of almost $1 billion in 1990 — to return to its **CORE COMPETENCIES** in retail markets and its strong consumer franchises based on its charge cards, American Express travel-related services, and IDS financial planning services. American Express continues to dispose of those businesses that do not fit into these categories.

## ANTIDUMPING

Government action, duties, or quotas to counteract **DUMPING**, the selling of goods in a foreign market below their cost of manufacture or at a lower price than in their home market.

Dumping is difficult to identify. One must find out the basis for a company's pricing policy, and determine whether that price represents the fair full cost of producing the item.

The Japanese are believed to be the world's greatest dumpers, selling all sorts of things — from photocopiers in Europe to semiconductors in America — at prices that have provoked retaliation in the form of import quotas and tariffs.

These controls have been at least partly responsible for the enormous growth in **FOREIGN DIRECT INVESTMENT (FDI)** by the Japanese in Europe and America in recent years. The Japanese have felt compelled to manufacture (more expensively) in these places in order to sell their products to those markets that have charged them with dumping. Companies competing with the Japanese in these markets will have to change their strategies subtly to cope with the changed nature of the competition. For one thing, they will be facing more predictable (and visible) rivals.

### Antitrust

The rules and laws that help maintain competition and suppress monopolies. The Sherman Antitrust Act of 1890, for example, makes price fixing among rivals illegal. Most antitrust laws, however, home in on mergers and on preventing monopoly by takeover. Any company pursuing a strategy of growth by **TAKEOVER** must be very well aware of antitrust laws.

In Europe antitrust rules now have more than just a national dimension: the European Commission (EC) has the right to examine large takeovers to see whether they have monopoly implications.

Monopoly can mean something less than 100% of a market. The U.S. government balked at allowing COCA-COLA to take over Dr Pepper and PEPSICO to take over 7-Up in deals that would have given the two cola giants over 80% of the U.S. soft-drink market. As it is, they have two-thirds of it. (American authorities tend to use the HERFINDAHL INDEX to measure CONCENTRATION in a market.)

The European authorities, however, did not stop NES-TLÉ from taking over Perrier mineral water in a deal that left Nestlé and BSN, a big French food group, with over 75% of the French mineral-water market between them. The moral of these stories? Each takeover is different and considered differently on its merits.

The increasing interest in collaborative strategies and creation of industrywide consortia have resulted in a rethinking of the role of antitrust measures in an era of strategic cooperation.

### APPLE

A California computer company that made a name for itself by developing machines that are

- User-friendly. Apple's software windows are easy to learn and highly visual; it developed the use of the mouse, which enabled a whole range of people ill at ease with the standard QWERTY keyboard to gain access to computers.

- Niche-oriented. In the 1980s, the Apple Macintosh (Mac) became the market leader in the rapidly grow-ing area of desktop publishing (DTP). Originally strongest in the consumer and education markets, Apple has successfully penetrated the mixed-layer business markets formerly dominated by IBM.

For the 1990s, under marketing-oriented chairman John Sculley (formerly of PepsiCo), Apple completely changed strategic direction. It "refocused its resources to pursue an aggressive market-share strategy." Said Sculley, "We have one goal: industry leadership."

To help it to achieve that goal, the company

- reduced the time it took to bring new products to market;
- lowered the prices on its Mac products; and
- extended the Mac product line.

In the early 1990s, Apple introduced three new low-priced computers in as many months; expanded its distribution channels around the world — making Apple products available through mass merchandisers for the first time; and forged a long-term alliance to develop microprocessors with IBM.

Apple has made very effective use of STRATEGIC ALLIANCES to tap into new technologies and share development costs, using, for example, the miniaturization expertise of SONY to decrease the size of the PowerBook laptop computer and reduce development time. Apple has also paired with IBM and Motorola to develop RISC-based Macintosh products and a new open systems platform.

### ARBITRAGE

An expression first used in financial markets, where it refers to the ability of a dealer to take advantage of price differences in different markets — buying yen, say, in Tokyo, in order to sell them immediately for a profit in New York. As telecommunications improve, and as the world's major financial markets become more integrated, such arbitrage opportunities diminish.

## ARTHUR ANDERSEN

An accounting firm and parent company of Andersen Consulting, the world's biggest management consultancy (with revenues of some $2 billion a year worldwide). Founded in Chicago in 1913 by Arthur Andersen, who left Price Waterhouse to start the company.

Andersen has always taken a straightforward approach to its business. Its founder believed in "thinking straight and talking straight" with clients, and not dressing up unpalatable truths in incomprehensible euphemisms.

The company is imbued with a distinctive culture that spreads out from its substantial training center near Chicago — to which come thousands of consultants from all 50 countries in which the firm operates for regular refresher courses.

Andersen recognized early on that its consultancy business was going to be enormously influenced by the development of the computer. Even in the early 1950s, it set up a model to show how businesses could make use of computers. Subsequently it built an unrivaled reputation in information technology — in recommending particular systems to corporations, in assembling them, and even in running them once installed.

For the 1990s, Andersen Consulting is putting much faith in a new service which it describes as Change Management — the process of designing jobs and systems (and of training people) so that they can be flexible enough to bend with the strong winds forecast for the business future.

> *The world is full of advice.*
> *What's in short supply is solutions.*
> Keith Burgess, Arthur Andersen

## ARTHUR D. LITTLE

A consulting firm that claims to be the world's oldest. It was founded in 1886 by then-23-year-old Arthur Dehon Little, a student at MIT, on the back of a contract to help New England paper mills to find new chemicals to break down their pulp. Until the early 1970s MIT was a major shareholder. Then Arthur D. Little briefly became a public company before being bought out by its employees.

The firm has deep technological roots: one of its first major consultancy projects was setting up an R&D department for GENERAL MOTORS. The firm has research facilities at Cambridge, Massachusetts, in the United States and at Cambridge, England. It is famous for thinking about strategy in terms of life cycles — a company's LIFE CYCLE (embryonic, growing, mature, aging) is plotted against its competitive position (dominant, strong, favorable, tenable, or weak). On this matrix the positions of each STRATEGIC BUSINESS UNIT is shown in order to give an overall picture of the company's strategic position.

Arthur D. Little's strength lies in its well-balanced mix between technology-based work (40%) and general management work (60%). A deep and broad range of technological expertise enables the firm to help clients formulate and implement technology strategies.

## Asea Brown Boveri (ABB)

The Swiss-Swedish conglomerate — the result of a 1988 merger between Switzerland's Brown Boveri and Sweden's Asea, one of the largest European cross-border mergers ever seen. The huge multinational is a world leader in electrical engineering and power-plant construction, and its strategy is to consolidate its range of businesses while broadening its geographical spread. Twenty years ago, a company engaged in such a large number of mature industries as ABB would have been advised to diversify into new EMERGENT INDUSTRIES. Nowadays it is advised to stick to its knitting.

ABB has been a pioneer in internationalization. Its chairmanship rotates between a Swede and a Swiss, and the official language of the company (and of its board) is English.

## Asset stripping

The purchase of a company followed by an immediate sale of almost all its assets — for a tidy profit. Asset stripping works when the market value of a company's stock is worth less than the sum of its parts. More than almost any other, this practice has antagonized the general public and turned it against entrepreneurs.

Much of the antagonism toward asset strippers lies in the claims they make in persuading shareholders to sell — claims that have on occasion involved long-term unfulfilled commitments. If no such disingenuous claims are made, asset stripping is no more than a STRATEGY that relies on market imperfections to increase profitability.

*I'm not asset-stripping . . .*
*I prefer to think of it as unbundling.*
Sir James Goldsmith at the time of his attempted takeover
of B.A.T. Industries

## AT&T

American Telephone & Telegraph, the large and monop-
olistic telecommunications company (once affection-
ately known as Ma Bell) that was forced to tear itself
apart (into a number of different companies known as
Baby Bells) in a hot flush of enthusiasm for antitrust
legislation in 1984.

AT&T emerged with two businesses: communication, consisting of long-distance telephone service and
dedicated high-speed data lines for business, and equipment manufacturing. After the breakup AT&T un-
derwent massive cultural change to become more
customer-oriented and efficient in a newly competitive market. AT&T's struggles, both before and after the
breakup, has provided a nice livelihood for the armies
of consultants it hired over the years.

AT&T's strategy is to gain COMPETITIVE ADVANTAGE
at the intersection of computer and telecommunications technologies. Its attempts to enter the computer
industry were unsuccessful, while the 1991 acquisition
of NCR provided a much-needed capability in computer
manufacturing, which AT&T is expected to apply to
electronic transaction processing.

## AUDIT COMMITTEE

A subcommittee of a company's **BOARD**, usually consisting only of nonexecutive directors and set up for the specific task of approving the audit and considering the reappointment (or otherwise) of the auditors.

Audit committees became extremely popular in the late 1980s with the realization that a number of corporate scandals and collapses were not helped by an over-cozy relationship between the collapsed company and its "reappointed-on-the-nod" auditors. Opponents of audit committees argue that they undermine the strength of the unitary board, talking and acting as a single team on all issues.

## AUTHORITY

A company's gift to its managers — to be used or abused. What enables them to take action on behalf of their company and to compel others to take action too.

With authority comes responsibility. The more widespread is authority throughout an organization, the more widespread is responsibility. (See also **AGENTS AND PRINCIPALS**)

## B

## BAIN & COMPANY

Bain was founded in 1973 when Bill Bain and a handful of colleagues left **THE BOSTON CONSULTING GROUP**. A highly secretive company, Bain has typically taken on long-term assignments with leading firms in a variety of industries. Working directly with their clients' CEOs, large teams of young, intensely loyal, professional MBAs analyze the details of the organizations, substituting their efforts for that of internal staff and making strategic recommendations at the top level.

Bain's emphasis is on measurable results. The company has calculated the increased market value of clients, a calculation that Bill Bain has shown to marketing prospects. Bain himself left the firm in 1991, at which point the firm experienced significant attrition as it restructured under the leadership of a new group of young professionals.

## BARRIER TO ENTRY (ENTRY BARRIER)

When a company decides to go into a new market it very rarely goes straight into virgin territory. Other firms already grazing in the meadow will have tried to protect their positions by erecting barriers to keep out new competitors.

These barriers may be no more offensive than **ECONOMIES OF SCALE**, high capital requirements, or loyal buyers. Entry barriers may arise from a patent on a particular process needed for the product in question, or they may result from the lack of a suitable site on which to start a new rival business (particularly relevant in retailing).

Once a firm has surmounted the barriers and entered the market, it is time for it to think of building its own barriers. One of the surest is to offer a highly differentiated product or to add new features and services that in effect redefine the industry. This might involve heavy investment in advertising (to establish a strong brand name) or securing exclusive arrangements with existing distributors that will make it much harder for new entrants to set up their own distribution network. For many years, IBM's large installed base of mainframe computers served as a powerful barrier to entry until advances in technology, including the minicomputer and later the PC, changed the basis of COMPETITION.

Other things being equal, an industry with high barriers to entry should be highly profitable.

### BARRIER TO EXIT (EXIT BARRIER)

The ease with which competitors can leave an industry strongly influences the profitability of that industry. High exit barriers keep a company in an industry even when it is not earning money. Exit barriers include specialized or fixed assets, interrelationships with related businesses, or even emotional ties.

These barriers have to be considered by firms as they enter new markets — not only as the downside for themselves should they fail in that market, but also as something preventing other firms from bowing out gracefully at the whiz-bang-wallop of the new entrant. For example, a firm may invest in totally new plant and equipment that produce goods far more efficiently than the existing manufacturer's outdated machinery does. But if the manufacturer's old plant has been fully depreciated, then it may base its prices on variable costs only.

The newcomer has to price goods on full costing. This unprofitable situation can continue long enough for the newcomer to have to give up before the original firm does.

### BENCHMARKING

Improving competitive position through a deliberate attempt to emulate and surpass what is considered to be world-class performance in important competitive activities.

Successful benchmarking requires the following:

- Identifying what to benchmark — choose activities that are crucial to competitive advantage.
- Identifying who to benchmark — do not limit the field to competitors. Xerox went to L.L. Bean to study order processing.
- Measuring your own performance.
- Identifying specific programs and practices to adopt and developing an implementation plan.

### BOARD

Company boards have a number of responsibilities that differ slightly in different cultures. In Anglo-Saxon economies they are primarily:

- to monitor management,
- to be a sounding board for STRATEGY,
- to appoint the CHIEF EXECUTIVE OFFICER,
- to decide on the rules by which the company will be governed and judged (corporate governance).

Executive directors will, almost by definition, be involved in formulating company strategy. But several advantages may be gained from involving nonexecutive directors in strategy sessions as well.

- It educates them about the company and its industry, and thereby increases the value of their future contributions.

- It brings a broader perspective to bear on strategy decisions.

- It gives the board background information that might be essential for making snap decisions later (about a potentially interesting acquisition, for example).

---

*The value that the board can add to the corporation stems from the breadth and independence of judgment that can be exercised by a group of experienced professionals who are, themselves, removed from direct operational responsibility.*

Ada Demb, IMD

---

## THE BODY SHOP

The most successful company to have come out of the so-called green movement. Founded by Anita Roddick, the daughter of an Italian immigrant to England who opened a small shop in a sleepy Sussex town, The Body Shop has grown on the back of

- the rising demand for bodycare products,
- stylish design, and
- increasing concern for the damage to the environment caused by traditional cosmetics manufacturers.

The Body Shop now has stores in over 40 countries, most of them operated as franchises, all of them selling the company's green products. The company's management and marketing are extremely unconventional. It never advertises, deeply distrusts banks, and printed the following in big letters on the back of its 1992 annual report:

> *Learn to love change. Feel comfortable with your creative intuition. Make compassion, care, harmony and trust the foundation stones of business. Fall in love with new ideas.*

### Booz, Allen & Hamilton

One of the oldest management consulting firms still in existence, Booz, Allen & Hamilton started life as a market research company in Chicago in 1914. It grew dramatically in World War II when it worked for the U.S. Navy on improving weapon-production systems.

It is now a major strategy consultancy, measuring itself against the market leader, MCKINSEY. In recent years the firm has hitched its wagon to the globalization star, setting up offices and working in more than 60 countries in the belief that such coverage is what its clients will increasingly demand. (See also PERT)

### The Boston Consulting Group (BCG)

Prominent management consulting firm, the first of a series of "strategy boutiques," founded just over 30 years ago by the late Bruce Henderson, an engineer by training. BCG (as it is commonly called) made its mark with the GROWTH SHARE MATRIX, originally developed by Henderson. With its "cash cows," "dogs," "stars," and "question marks," the GSM was one of the most catchy frameworks ever designed for strategic thinking (in this case about the allocation of scarce capital resources). Like all catchy ideas, however, its novelty eventually wore off.

In the 1960s and 1970s, BCG was at the forefront of the fashion for company DIVERSIFICATION. The growth share matrix provided a framework for the management of just such a portfolio of businesses. BCG also emphasized the importance of high market share, and popularized the idea of the EXPERIENCE CURVE.

The firm's latest contribution to the field of strategy, as well as an important source of consulting revenues, is TIME-BASED COMPETITION.

---

*Darwin is probably a better guide to business competition than economists are.*

Bruce Henderson of BCG

---

## BP

Once known as British Petroleum and once 22%-owned by the Kuwaitis, BP is one of the two European members of the so-called Seven Sisters — the seven companies that for many years monopolized the oil research and distribution business throughout the world. (The others were ROYAL DUTCH/SHELL, EXXON, Mobil, Texaco, Gulf, and Chevron. In 1984, Chevron bought Gulf, and the seven became six.)

In 1990, BP chose a new CHAIRMAN and CHIEF EXECUTIVE OFFICER, a feisty Scot named Bob Horton, who set about trimming staff and chasing after new exploration

— much of it in harsh parts of the world such as Colombia and newly non-Communist Azerbaijan.

However, "Hatchet Horton" was unable to turn the company around fast enough. Following a traumatic loss by BP in the first quarter of 1992, the unpopular boss was forced to resign. After his resignation, the jobs of chairman and chief executive were (wisely) split between two people.

### BRAINSTORMING

A technique in use for over 50 years in which a number of people get together in an unstructured setting and attempt to come up with new ideas or new solutions to problems. The first aim is to generate as many ideas as possible; only later (or maybe even at a different session) are the ideas in any way evaluated.

### BRAND DEVELOPMENT INDEX (BDI)

A measure of a product's penetration of different parts of a market. For example, if TOYOTA has 7.3% of its American sales in an area that contains 10% of the American population, then Toyota's BDI for that area is said to be 73.

A BDI of over 100 indicates a region where the product sells particularly well. Knowledge of different BDIs can help a company decide where to focus its MARKETING and advertising efforts.

*The strength of our brands begins with our people.*

Slogan of Philip Morris, owner of Kraft, Marlboro, and Maxwell House

## BRANDING

The creation of a strong (that is, trusted) name or trademark for a product or service through mass advertising. Branding has become big business as companies realize what valuable assets names can be: names like AMERICAN EXPRESS or Pampers. Consumers will pay a premium to cover their babies' bottoms with diapers they can trust. This premium can be seen as the income flowing from the capital value of the brand name.

The benefits of strong branding are widespread. It is easier to launch a new product with a known brand name than to launch one with an unknown name. (Nevertheless, many companies prefer to launch new products with entirely new brand names. PROCTER & GAMBLE manufactures 14 different types of laundry detergent, for example; Reckitt & Colman produces Colman's mustard as well as French's mustard — and Airwick air freshener.)

A branding strategy needs to be supported by every function in the organization. Manufacturing must provide consistent and adequate quality. MARKETING must project a consistent message, and distribution channels must be appropriate.

A new product that is not acceptable to the consumer can undermine the value of the brand name on the old product. The value of a brand name alone, however, should not be overestimated.

## BREAK-EVEN ANALYSIS

A product breaks even when sales revenue equals the fixed and variable costs of producing it. Additional sales volume is profit. The key calculation lies in identifying all fixed costs (plant and equipment, advertising, promotion, and so forth) and variable costs (e.g., labor and materials) actually associated with the product.

Comparing projected break-even volume to estimated total market size establishes the **MARKET SHARE** that the product must achieve to become profitable. This is a good reality check on sales objectives and the risk involved in a new venture.

### BRITISH AIRWAYS (BA)

The British flag-carrier that likes to call itself "The World's Favorite Airline." BA's **MISSION STATEMENT** says that it aims "to be the best and most successful company in the airline industry." Time will tell whether its recent merger with USAir will move the company closer to or further from this goal.

In the 1980s British Airways went a long way toward achieving that. Under the firm hand of its chairman Lord King (a close ally of Mrs. Thatcher), it turned substantial losses into big profits as it left the public sector and was privatized. It even made a profit in the Gulf War year of 1991, a feat that scarcely any other airline matched.

Lord King tolerated neither fools nor competitors gladly and seemed willing to compromise his free-market principles to ensure that BA's duopoly on most worthwhile routes was not challenged. The real test for the airline will come when European airlines are fully deregulated. A similar exercise in the United States reduced the number of profitable big airlines here to three or four. Europe can still boast about more than 20 large national airlines.

British Airways' turnabout began with a training program designed to give its staff a customer-oriented culture. This was distilled into seven company goals:

1. To be safe and secure
2. To be financially strong
3. To be a global leader
4. To give good service and value for money
5. To be customer driven
6. To be a good employer
7. To be a good neighbor (that is, to care for the environment at least as much as the airline next door)

### Bubble chart

A ubiquitous business graphic and consultant's stock in trade is a matrix on which businesses, companies, or products are represented by circles (bubbles) proportional in size to a measure of competitive strength such as sales, assets, or MARKET SHARE. Use of bubbles introduces a third measure to a two-dimensional matrix. (See GROWTH SHARE MATRIX)

### Budgeting

If proof were needed that business and family life are not far apart, then it lies in the obsession of both with budgeting. Budgeting is the way in which the financial constraints on families and managers are brought to bear on STRATEGY.

One of the main dangers of budgeting is ossification — last year's budget is simply reproduced this year, with 5% or 10% added on. The family budgeted to take the children to the shore for two weeks last year. So it does the same for this year. But it forgot that the children are now well into their teens and fed up with buckets and spades. They want to spend a week in London or New York with their friends, and without their parents — an entirely different financial proposition. The same will be true in a less blatant way for managers and the products or brands for which they are responsible.

This problem has led to the growing popularity of ZERO-BASE BUDGETING.

### BUSINESS ATTRACTIVENESS/INDUSTRY STRENGTH MATRIX

Also known as the McKinsey/GE screen, a technique first used by GENERAL ELECTRIC to evaluate its diverse businesses. A range of factors determines business strength (or competitive position) and industry attractiveness. Not surprisingly, diversified companies are advised to build strong business in attractive industries. The matrix is similar to the GROWTH SHARE MATRIX. Unlike BCG's matrix, however, the McKinsey/GE screen includes a variety of subjective factors. On the one hand this renders the screen less quantitative, but on the other it can include more subtle determinants of strength and attractiveness.

### BUSINESS CYCLE

Economic growth is not a smooth uninterrupted process; it goes in cycles. Those cycles vary in length, with at least one Russian economist (Kondratieff) delineating a background of long cycles ranging from 50 to 60 years, against which shorter ups and downs were set.

Clement Juglar, the Frenchman who first spotted the shorter business cycles in the 1860s, concluded (on the basis of evidence from his native France, and from Britain and the United States) that the short cycles averaged between 8 and 10 years and argued that they were an inevitable consequence of capitalism.

The nature of the business cycle can best be seen by considering a single industry — say, shipping. When trade grows, shipping companies increase their freight charges because there is more demand for the space on their ships. The increase in freight charges then persuades the shippers to build more ships in order to meet the extra demand. But it takes a long time to build a ship, and by the time one is in the water so are those of competitors that have thought in exactly the same way. So freight prices then fall, and so do the number of shippers prepared to order new ships.

The clever company is the one that spots a business cycle in its very earliest stages and then invests rapidly. Not only does that make it ready to reap the benefit at the peak of the cycle, but a forceful early move might pre-exempt rivals from doing the same.

### BUSINESS PLAN

One of the first steps in starting any new business venture is the preparation of a business plan, a document that sets out in words and figures a projection of how the new business (or the expansion of an old business) is going to proceed. The business plan has three main purposes:

1. It gives the proposers a way of clarifying their thoughts by compelling them to put those thoughts on paper.

2. It helps persuade banks or investors to put money into the venture.

**3.** It provides checks along the way, both as and after the project gets started.

There is no single prescribed format for a business plan. But all must contain information about the market for the proposed product; about the product or service to be offered; about the proposed staff and their qualifications; about the premises and equipment from which the product is to be produced or the service delivered; and the financial details, including a carefully considered forecast of CASH FLOW, a projection of future profits and losses, and financing requirements.

For ongoing businesses, the business plan (or annual plan) is an integral part of the strategic planning process; in it, STRATEGY is translated into tactics or specific action steps for the business unit.

### BUSINESS PROCESS

A series of activities that deliver value to a customer — for example, order fulfillment and credit issuance. Business processes are collections of activities or tasks that typically span different departments and functional units in the traditional corporation. The goal of business process thinking is to overcome the inefficiencies, redundancies, and divided loyalties that result from a task focus in a traditional organization. A process orientation focuses attention on what needs to be done to add value and how best to do it. Business process thinking is a fundamental element in REENGINEERING.

### BUSINESS UNIT

See STRATEGIC BUSINESS UNIT

## Cannibalize

To market a new product or service that knowingly eats into the market of another product or service. When Heinz introduced its canned spaghetti in the shape of letters of the alphabet, it knows it is going to reduce the sales of its main line of straightforward canned spaghetti. Smart companies cannabalize their own products before their competitors do.

The reasons for cannibalizing a product may be strategically sound: to meet new **COMPETITION** for the children's share of the canned spaghetti market, for example, or to deter such competition from entering the market. But the cannibalizer runs the risk of destroying the product being cannibalized. For example, if children are the whole market for canned spaghetti, then they may stop eating the straightforward variety altogether.

## Canon

The remarkable Japanese company that revolutionized the production and marketing of the photographic camera, and then went on to grab market leadership of the competitive photocopying industry. The company is now highly innovative, and in 1991 marketed the world's first full-color fax machine.

The company was for long spurred on by a simple yet apposite **MISSION STATEMENT** that the Japanese seem to be particularly expert at framing: "Beat Xerox," the great American inventor of photocopying. (See **STRATEGIC INTENT**)

Canon is now focusing strongly on being a model corporation in terms of its concern for the environment and for the quality of life of its employees. "We are determined that none of Canon's products or activities will be harmful to humans or the environment," it says.

## CAPACITY

The quantity of goods that a factory or machine can produce within a certain time period. Managers have devised a number of useful different concepts of capacity:

- Ideal or maximum capacity — sometimes referred to as full capacity — is the level of activity that would be attained if circumstances were ideal.
- Practical capacity is the operating level that is reasonable to expect, given the time lost for repairs to equipment, for holidays, and so on.
- Normal capacity is the average level of production needed to fulfill existing demand for the company's output.
- Excess capacity is the amount of extra volume that a firm could produce if all its existing plant and equipment were fully used 24 hours a day. More recently the expression has been applied to "softer" assets that are underutilized (for example, brand names and management systems).

## CAPITAL BUDGETING

The process of allocating a company's capital between competing divisions and investment proposals. The traditional method of doing this has been to choose those investments that look set to give the highest (discounted) RATE OF RETURN.

Such pure financial considerations, however, have their shortcomings:

- There is the intrinsic difficulty of being precise about the underlying assumptions in any calculation of a future rate of return. If in the end the mathematical method is inaccurate, why not try other methods?
- Other strategic considerations can override financial ones, at least in the short term. A company may want to establish itself in a particular market simply to keep competitors out. Again, it may need to pour capital into a new technology that has a measureless potential — but only in the distant future.

The financial approach tends to consider each investment proposal in isolation. Many now prefer to set capital budgeting in a wider context. Models such as the GROWTH SHARE MATRIX emphasize the portfolio nature of a company's businesses and their interdependence.

### CAPITAL INTENSITY

The amount of capital, usually in the form of fixed assets, needed to run a business. It is usually measured as the ratio of fixed assets to total sales. Capital intensity makes it difficult to enter an industry and difficult to leave. Competition becomes intense as a consequence.

### CAPTIVE

A wholly owned subsidiary that carries out the financial functions a company would traditionally buy from outside, such as insurance or consumer credit. GMAC, a subsidiary of GENERAL MOTORS, provides consumer credit for the purchase of GM's products; other companies own offshore insurance businesses that cover the risks of the whole group.

Only the very largest companies can contemplate having their own captives, and even then the costs and benefits need to be carefully assessed. It may be only a temporary aberration of the market that enables them to provide such services more cheaply themselves.

## CAREER

*"Career planning" and "career path" convey the impression of an orderly accumulation of required skills and attitudes that lead to a specified destination. Recent experience in firms that are facing competitive shifts and internal changes suggests that a successful path cannot be a gentle slope with clearly marked way stations.*

*Rather, that the process is more like an irregular ratchet effect, where the boss jolts promising subordinates out of a comfortable groove into a troubling challenge, and some of them have the fortitude and learning capacity to attain a new foothold — until they are faced with the next bump.*

J.B.M. Kassarjian
Professor of Management, Babson College

## CARTEL

A group of firms in the same line of business that colludes in setting prices. The most famous cartel is OPEC (the Organization of Petroleum Exporting Countries). Because of its control over the world's oil supplies, OPEC was able to fix the price of oil more or less at whatever level it wished. Its power, however, has waned in recent years, for at least three reasons:

- Oil has been found in places outside OPEC that are not bound by its price rules.
- OPEC has encouraged consumers to develop and use alternative forms of fuel.
- It has proved hard at times to keep all members of the cartel in line. When demand for oil is high, they stick together; when it is not, the weaker members are tempted to give special offers in order to maintain their revenues. No cartel can be stronger than its weakest member.

In many parts of the world cartels are illegal. Nevertheless they continue to exist in secret in many industries. (Trustbusters commonly find them in the chemical, pharmaceutical, and financial industries.)

Part of the identification problem is that the behavior of a cartel can, in many respects, resemble the behavior of a market under conditions of perfect competition. For example, when a number of banks change their interest rates identically at the same time on the same day, who is to say that they don't do this because competition is fierce and they cannot afford to be out of line for more than a morning? One bank CHAIRMAN, however, may have called the others, given them a series of coded messages, and all acted as a cartel.

## CASH COW

A type of business occupying the bottom left-hand corner of BCG's GROWTH SHARE MATRIX. A cash cow is a business with a high market share but low-growth prospects. Companies are advised to use the cash produced by their cash cows to support their stars and their question marks (the company businesses that have high-growth potential).

This idea seemed radical in its time because the temptation for managers is often to reinvest the surplus cash into the cash cow itself — as a sort of reward for success. It feels intuitively wrong to "milk" a successful business in order to feed an as-yet unproven one.

The danger now, perhaps, is the other way round: managers have become so familiar with the thinking behind the Growth Share Matrix that they always starve the cash cow, ignoring any potential it still has for rejuvenation. There is an additional problem in persuading able managers that a business already identified as a cash cow — good only for milking — is good enough for them to devote their full attention to it.

## CASH FLOW

The amount of cash coming into a business during a specified period of time. Not to be confused with profit or net income, cash flow refers to cash revenues and disbursements only. Important noncash items such as accounts payable, receivables, depreciation, and the like determine profitability but not cash flow. In many countries the annual financial statement must include a report of the company's cash flow during the year, along with the income statement and the balance sheet. It is the third most significant corporate financial statement.

A strong cash flow has advantages and disadvantages. On the one hand, it is a strong indication of a company's continued ability to conduct business and it releases the firm from the exacting demands of the capital markets; on the other hand, it raises the vexing question of what to do with it. There are three alternatives:

1. Invest it in other businesses that have high demand for cash. This has led to many a disastrous **DIVERSI-FICATION** in the past. Too many companies have assumed that management is fungible — that it can be spread around any business willy-nilly.

2. Keep it so that it earns interest. In this case the company is behaving like a bank, which is probably not what its shareholders would wish. But this option has proved popular because companies are strangely reluctant to follow the third alternative.

3. Distribute the surplus cash back to shareholders either in the form of dividends or as more tax-efficient capital redistributions. If capital markets were truly efficient, this is what would happen. Shareholders would then be free to reinvest their money as they saw fit.

---

*Every set of published accounts is based on books which have been gently cooked or completely roasted. The figures which are fed twice a year to the investing public have all been changed to protect the guilty. It is the biggest con trick since the Trojan horse.*

Ian Griffiths, *Creative Accounting*

### CATERPILLAR

The manufacturer of earth-moving equipment that found its home base — Peoria, Illinois — left it out of touch with the rest of the world during the globalization of the 1980s.

It began the decade as a giant of the industry, with annual sales of over $9 billion and profits of over $500 million. Then as the third-world debt crisis and high interest rates slashed its turnover by a third, it became the victim of a famous Japanese corporate MISSION STATEMENT — that of a minor rival called Komatsu, which (incredibly) was determined to "Encircle Caterpillar." And it did.

In 1991, Caterpillar's sales were still just over $9 billion, and it was sustaining huge losses. It cut staff and plant so ruthlessly that it received the censure of a senior government minister in the United Kingdom. Trying to turn itself around, it went through a painful internal reorganization that decentralized the company away from Peoria and set up a form of MATRIX MANAGEMENT when many companies were disbanding theirs (see PHILIPS).

Caterpillar chairman Donald Fites said:

*Caterpillar is undergoing an unprecedented level of culture change as decision-making is pushed down to lower levels, and divisions are held accountable for the actions they take. Each profit center division is being measured against a comprehensive set of performance criteria, the most critical of which is return on assets.*

### CENTRALIZATION

The process of concentrating AUTHORITY at the center of an organization — usually at its headquarters. The

advantage to be gained from this in terms of control —
and, maybe, ECONOMIES OF SCALE — is outweighed by
the disadvantages of inflexibility and of the removal of
authority from the lower rungs of the hierarchical
ladder.

Centralization was popular with the raw efficiency
experts whose thinking dominated management until
the 1970s. With the recent switch of emphasis to softer
sides of management — for example, CORPORATE CUL-
TURE and EMPLOYEE INVOLVEMENT — centralization has
become the victim of fashion. The truth is probably that
certain functions are best centralized; others are better
for being pushed away from the center. In UNILEVER, for
example, the DECENTRALIZATION of operational decision
making is high, but strategic decision making is still
very centralized.

Some advantages of decentralization:

- It speeds up decision making.
- It enhances the commitment of line managers.
- It reduces the need for paper-pushing middle man-
  agement.

Some potential disadvantages of decentralization:

- It can make line managers averse to change.
- It can squander savings that could be made from combining aspects of different parts of the business.
- It reduces the control of top management over operations (but that may not be a disadvantage).

### CHAIRMAN

Titles matter, and the higher up the organization that
people get, the more they matter. But titles mean different things in different countries. Confusing the signals
given out by different titles can make business difficult.

This is one business term that so far has successfully resisted efforts to promote gender-neutral terminology.

- In the United States, the chairman also tends to be the **CHIEF EXECUTIVE OFFICER**.
- In the United Kingdom, the chairman is more frequently a nonexecutive; and the chief executive is called the **MANAGING DIRECTOR**.

Many gurus prefer to see the roles split, believing that one man (it is almost always a man) should not have to bear the double burden of being chief representative of the interests of shareholders (as chairman) and those of management (as chief executive).

- In Germany companies have two chairmen because they have two **BOARDS**. One is an executive chairman (head of the managing board), and one is a nonexecutive chairman (head of the supervisory board). This can be confusing to non-Germans. For example, Alfred Herrhausen (assassinated by terrorists in 1991) was often described as the chairman of **DEUTSCHE BANK** (Germany's most powerful financial institution) and chairman of **DAIMLER-BENZ** (Germany's most powerful industrial corporation). In fact he was executive chairman of the bank's managing board and nonexecutive chairman of Daimler-Benz's supervisory board.
- In Japanese companies the **PRESIDENT** is the boss; in American companies the president is often number two, the equivalent of the deputy chairman or vice chairman in a British company.

## CHANGE

Management has become increasingly focused on how to manage change. It represents a crucial switch from viewing corporations as static entities (or at least as entities in search of a static state) to seeing them as dynamic organizations in a constant state of flux. Much management thinking has been based on assumptions that apply only to the static state — much of long-term planning, for example.

Learning to live with change is somehow counterintuitive. Managers are almost always conservative and, by definition, abhor change. Their abhorrence is born mostly of fear — the fear of failure and the fear of going beyond a point of no return.

---

*There is at least one point in the history of any company when you have to change dramatically to rise to the next performance level. Miss that moment and you start to decline.*

Andrew Grove of Intel (*Fortune*, May 3, 1993, p. 39)

---

### CHANNEL OF DISTRIBUTION

The route by which a finished product passes from the factory gate to the final consumer. Most manufacturers will have several channels of distribution. Coordinating them so that they do not overlap too much is an important task for the manufacturer, and ensuring a good fit between the product, its positioning in the market, and the distribution channel are important aspects of channel strategy. It is also important that the manufacturer use these channels as much as possible to read what is happening in its markets — taking information in from them is as useful as giving products out to them.

### CHANNEL PARTNERSHIPS

A STRATEGIC ALLIANCE between two companies to create COMPETITIVE ADVANTAGE in distribution or sales.
Thanks to breakthroughs in information and telecommunications technologies, the benefits of VERTICAL
INTEGRATION can now be achieved without the costs
associated with ownership and control. Channel partnerships involve REENGINEERING between companies,
typically focused on such business processes as product
delivery and customer service. Reengineering elimi-
nates duplicate steps between the customer order and
the supplier's fulfillment, or between receipt and payment (see WAL-MART).

### CHIEF EXECUTIVE OFFICER (CEO)

The head manager. The CEO's involvement and commitment are key to almost every successful strategic
move a corporation makes. (See CHAIRMAN and MANAG-
ING DIRECTOR)

### CHIEF OPERATING OFFICER (COO)

The manager in charge of the day-to-day running of the
organization — as opposed to the CHIEF EXECUTIVE OFFI-
CER, who is responsible for more lofty things such as
strategy.

### CITICORP

A mighty New York-based bank that managed to grow
streets ahead of its rivals in the 1980s. Under its charis-
matic chief executive, Walter Wriston, it grew in three
directions.

- It took new opportunities to spread outside New York state.

- It moved as far as it could into investment banking.

- It spread its wings into every possible overseas market it could find, buying stockbrokers in many countries and insurance businesses in others.

These actions gave it a size and breadth that no other institution could match. However, when Walter Wriston was followed by John Reed, his hand-picked baby-faced successor, things went badly wrong. In 1991, the company had losses of $450 million and instituted a plan for recovery that featured the following five points:

1. Examine closely every aspect of the bank's operations around the world.

2. Manage differently; to reduce the cost base and improve the revenue/expense ratio.

3. Strengthen the capital base.

4. Build on the strengths of its core businesses.

5. Maintain a strong customer focus.

### CLONE

A word taken from biology, where it means a genetically identical copy of an organism. In business a clone is a product that for all intents and purposes is indistinguishable from one already on the market. Such products are often found in the computer industry. IBM's first personal computers, for example, contained no proprietary technology and were rapidly copied by lower-cost manufacturers. The success of the clone manufacturers' STRATEGY depended on convincing customers that they really were getting the same QUALITY as an IBM machine for a lower price.

Where a product is protected by copyright or intellectual property rights, a clone may become a COUNTER-FEIT.

### Coca-Cola

Coke may well be the most familiar brand name in the entire world. Available in 195 countries worldwide, it is viewed as an icon of American culture.

Coca-Cola continues to focus on international growth, particularly in developing countries. Under CEO Roberto Goizueta, Coca-Cola had returned to the basics by divesting itself of holdings in wine, coffee, tea, water treatment, and agriculture, and by selling Columbia Pictures to Sony. Goizueta's objective is to increase SHAREHOLDER WEALTH: since he took over as CEO in 1980, the company's market value has grown from $4 billion to approximately $56 billion today.

At one point, Coca-Cola defined its business as selling syrup to bottlers. Today the company owns or controls the bottlers themselves.

---

*We used to be an American company with a large international business. Now we're a large international company with a sizable American business.*

Robert Goizueta (*Fortune*, May 31, 1993, p. 52)

---

### Co-Determination

A reference to various systems in which representatives of employees are actively involved in making decisions about their company's STRATEGY. These can range from the German system of having worker directors on company boards to the participative Japanese system in which employee committees at almost every level have their views fed into the general decision-making maw.

## COMPETITION

The underlying operating principle of capitalist business — that products be provided to markets in a contest where the producer of the best value for the money wins. Those who come in second and third also thrive, but the rest usually have to live in constant struggle.

A key issue for any business is how it can gain COMPETITIVE ADVANTAGE in the commercial competition for the favors of consumers. A less obvious (but increasingly important) issue for business lies in what is the ideal trade-off between competition and cooperation. Many a JOINT VENTURE is now formed between traditional rivals that find that in certain stages of the development of new products it is better to cooperate rather than to compete with rivals. Competition comes at a later stage. (See also CONSORTIUM)

---

*I don't meet competition. I crush it.*

Charles Revson, founder of Revlon

---

## COMPETITIVE ADVANTAGE

The surprisingly recent idea that a company's STRATEGY should focus on becoming stronger than one's competitors in an area that will allow the company to produce and deliver a product more efficiently or charge a higher price. Either will result in higher profits. A company is good at manufacturing when (and only when) it has a competitive advantage over other manufacturers. Such an advantage can lie in many things: lower costs because of greater computerization and lower wage bills, more reliable machinery, better quality control, cheaper borrowing, and so on.

The idea has led companies to pay more attention to comparing their performance with that of their rivals rather than with that old favorite — their own performance in a previous period. (See also **VALUE-ADDED**)

The earlier concepts of competitive advantage focused on the role of cost and market share as the sole determinants of competitive advantage. Michael Porter asserted that competitive advantage can arise from either low cost or the ability to differentiate a product in the eyes of customers and thereby command a premium price. Broadly speaking, a clever company should be able to tap diverse sources of competitive advantage through the activities in its **VALUE CHAIN**, and, by translating these into a superior product or a lower cost, achieve competitive advantage.

---

*The danger is that we draw up our plans on the basis of beating what our competitors are doing now, forgetting that they too are looking ahead. We have to devise strategies which will deliver a decisive advantage over what our competitors may have in mind. Competition is dynamic, and our strategic thinking has to be dynamic as well.*

Sir Adrian Cadbury, 1992

## COMPETITOR ANALYSIS

A surprising amount of information on corporate activity is publicly available. Financial information from annual reports and 10-Ks for publicly held corporations are easily accessible. Patents and patent applications (also public documents) reveal much about technology strategy. State, local, and federal environmental agencies require detailed information on raw materials, production processes, fuel consumption, and waste disposal. Although it may require some effort, this information is also publicly available and reveals much about manufacturing capability. Salepeople find out about competitors' products from current and potential customers in the routine course of doing business.

The trick is to put it all together. Competitor analysis requires piecing together bits of information gleaned from a variety of sources to reveal patterns and to make judgments about likely strategic moves. It is best done on an ongoing basis. To be effective, competitor analyses must be shared with appropriate decision makers.

## CONCENTRATION

The degree to which any particular industry is controlled by a few firms. This is usually measured by the percentage of the industry's total turnover that is in the hands of the four largest firms in the business (known as the C4 ratio), the five largest (known as the C5), or the eight largest firms (C8).

Another measure is the HERFINDAHL INDEX, which takes the square of the MARKET SHARE of each firm in the industry (expressed as a fraction), and adds them together. The closer they are to 1, the more dominant is the industry leader. (An index of 1 means that a single firm in the industry has a 100% market share.)

It is obviously important for companies to monitor concentration ratios in their own industry in order to discover whether their market is becoming an OLIGOP-OLY — in which case different strategies apply. But it is also important for them to follow whether their customers' (or their suppliers') industries are becoming more concentrated, for that will give them more or less power in their buying or selling.

## CONSORTIUM

An alliance for precompetitive research. In 1984, the Cooperative Research Act eliminated the risk of antitrust liability for this activity. Interest in collaborative research efforts was fueled by the high cost and complexity of basic research as well as a need to respond to international competition. Examples include MCC (the Microelectronics and Computer Technology Corporation), established in 1982; Sematech, a consortium of 14 U.S. electronics companies, founded in 1987 to restore American competitiveness in integrated circuit manufacturing technology; and ESPIRIT, a European consortium to develop information technology.

Consortia have had mixed success to date. Three important management issues have emerged:

- Divided loyalties of staff assigned to the consortium, who normally rotate from the member companies

- Reluctance to assign highly talented staff to projects

- Failure to develop mechanisms to further develop and commercialize the technology developed by the consortium within member companies

## Continuous improvement

English translation of Japanese term *kaizen*. The drive for continuous improvement, originally applied to manufacturing quality, has broadened in scope to include all business processes. The focus is on small but cumulative improvements that add up over time to substantial **COMPETITIVE ADVANTAGE.**

## Contrarian

A person who follows a **STRATEGY** contrary to everybody else's, especially in the stock market; contrarians will sell shares when everyone else is buying them. They do this not just to be different; their behavior is based on the logic that buyers will soon run out of purchasing power to buy more shares. They will then have to start selling, thus pushing prices down, after which they may be able to buy at a price that is lower than that at which they have sold.

Contrarians rely on sheep being wrong. But the wrongness of sheep is a matter of timing. Early sheep-like followers will find enough grass in the market on which to graze. The last sheep will not — and would be better off being a contrarian.

## Core competence

Competitive advantage, argue C. K. Prahalad and Gary Hamel in a *Harvard Business Review* article entitled "The Core Competence of the Corporation" (May–June 1990), comes from five or six fundamental competencies that they define as "the collective learning in the organization, especially how to coordinate diverse production skills and integrate multiple streams of technologies."

This skill enables a company to develop new products swiftly, enter new markets quickly, to become capable of "infusing products with irresistible functionality or, better yet, creating products that customers need, but have not even imagined." Examples are the expertise in miniaturization that Sony applies across a range of products, and Honda's core competence in engines and power trains, which gives it a distinct advantage in cars, motorcycles, lawn mowers, and generators.

Prahalad and Hamel describe three tests to identify core competence:

- Does it provide potential access to a wide variety of markets?

- Does it make a significant contribution to the perceived customer benefits of the end products?

- Is it difficult for competitors to imitate?

---

*Only when your aspirations and desires lie outside your resources does creativity occur, because you have to invent new ways of competing and change the rules of the game.*

C. K. Prahalad (*Business Week*, August 31, 1992, p. 46)

---

### CORNING INC.

For decades, the U.S. manufacturer of optical fiber, glass for television picture tubes and LCD displays, specialized ceramics, and the familiar Corning Ware, Pyrex, and Revere Ware kitchen products has successfully implemented state-of-the-art management practices. It made its first STRATEGIC ALLIANCE (really only a JOINT VENTURE) in 1924, and today almost 20 partnerships generate over a third of Corning's net income. These alliances allow Corning to develop and sell products faster, utilizing highly specialized technologies. Corning treats its partners as equals and attempts to understand their objectives to satisfy both sides' interests.

James R. Houghton, CEO of this family-controlled company, has embraced such concepts as QUALITY, EMPLOYEE INVOLVEMENT, MANAGING DIVERSITY, and SOCIAL RESPONSIBILITY. Observers credit the successful implementation of these programs to three generations of owner/managers, the Houghtons, who have enjoyed the luxury of being able to manage for the long term. Since 85% of the company's stock is publicly traded, Corning may be able to balance long- and short-term financial considerations better than most firms.

## CORPORATE CULTURE

The shared values, assumptions, and beliefs that shape the way things are done in an organization. Formed over years, and seldom explicit, corporate culture shapes management style, attitude toward risk, decision-making processes, and ultimately STRATEGY itself. Some organizations have highly visible cultures — IBM's was symbolized by employees' blue suits, white shirts, and their tendency to use their own jargon.

Corporate culture matters most when it becomes dysfunctional. CHANGE may be required

- when markets change;
- when competition changes;
- after an acquisition;

- to improve research and development, product development; and
- to improve quality service.

## CORPORATE PLANNING

A system for deciding how to allocate scarce resources between different parts of an organization — a system that was designed for the large diversified corporations built up in the 1960s and 1970s. In the heyday of corporate planning, **PORTFOLIO MANAGEMENT** techniques became popular approaches to the central task of corporate planning, which in turn encouraged the growth of **CENTRALIZATION** within these diversified corporations. But with the breakup of many conglomerates in the 1980s and the popularity of **DECENTRALIZATION**, the role of corporate planning has been much diminished in recent years.

## COST-BENEFIT ANALYSIS

The calculation of the benefit to customers accruing from a particular cost; for example, how much extra will consumers pay for guaranteed same-day postal delivery service from within the same city? Is the benefit to be gained from the premium price higher than the cost of setting up the service?

Cost-benefit analysis is not a difficult concept to grasp. The problem arises in deciding what costs to include in the analysis (should there be a contribution from the overhead costs of all the post office's services in the preceding example?) and what benefits (how do you measure the favorable feeling of customers toward the post office for a new service designed just for them?).

## COST CENTER

A unit to which the specific costs of a business can be allocated — this can be something as small as an individual machine. The importance of allocating costs correctly to different centers is an important prerequisite to the formation of any STRATEGY. If a company does not know where its costs arise, it does not know where its profits arise.

## COST LEADER

A firm that has a consistent cost advantage over its competitors in an industry. This is usually achieved by a widespread shaving of costs in all areas of production and distribution. It does not often come from a single dramatic cost advantage — for example, from finding a source of cheap raw materials. Such advantages are rarely enjoyed alone for long.

Any cost leader will owe its position in part to exploitation of ECONOMIES OF SCALE. Hence it needs to guard against competitors gaining substantial MARKET SHARE, for that will allow them to gain new economies of scale, and to threaten the cost leader's position.

## COST OF CAPITAL

A firm can gain considerable COMPETITIVE ADVANTAGE by structuring its capital in a way that will minimize its cost. The firm must consider whether the capital should be equity or debt, identify the relative cost of each, and determine the optimal balance between them.

After that a firm has to decide where to borrow. Large companies borrow in many different foreign capital markets. There they make a trade-off between interest-rate differentials and shifting rates of FOREIGN EXCHANGE.

Historically, Swiss interest rates have been low. But if Swiss franc interest payments have to be made out of revenues denominated in a weak currency, the extra currency to be paid over time to buy the same number of Swiss francs might well outweigh the benefit from the lower interest rates.

A firm uses its COST OF CAPITAL estimate to evaluate investment projects.

### COST STRUCTURE

The allocation of a company's costs between fixed, variable, and marginal. This allocation has a crucial bearing on a company's STRATEGY. A company with high fixed costs will have higher BARRIERS TO EXIT than will a company with lower fixed costs. That has implications for the company itself, and for all its competitors. It means, for example, that a company should beware of entering a market where all the participants have high fixed costs.

### COUNTERFEIT

There are few sensible ways to respond to widespread copying of well-known companies' products and services other than by an expensive pursuit of the counterfeiters through every available court and by an internationally coordinated attempt to force countries with weak copyright and patent laws to beef them up.

Some companies believe that widespread publicity can help. Cartier had photographers take pictures as it drove a bulldozer over a hoard of fake Cartier watches discovered in the Far East.

### CREDIT CONTROL

The process of controlling the amount of credit that a company grants to its customers in order to improve its

CASH FLOW and to reduce the value of its bad debts. A reduction of one day in the average outstanding period of a company's creditors can make the difference between a sound business and a wobbly one.

## CRISIS MANAGEMENT

Any company is vulnerable to a sudden disaster that threatens its whole business. For example, the poisonous gases that escaped from Union Carbide's plant at Bhopal in India, killing thousands of people in 1984. Or the small quantities of carcinogenic benzene found in Perrier's water source. Both were events that overnight threatened huge companies with disaster.

More than half of all large companies now have a contingency plan about what to do on the occasion of such a crisis. Here are the widely copied guidelines devised by one company (a subsidiary of Warner-Lambert).

- Look out for signs that may foretell a crisis.
- Have an alternative product or technology standing by.
- Remember that speed is of the essence; the first few days' behavior is vital.
- Don't overreact.
- Stay close to your market.
- Watch the competition's reaction.
- Be prepared to yield some of your market initially.
- Don't assume a hostile environment.
- Build GOODWILL before the crisis — it will stand you in good stead.

## CRITICAL PATH ANALYSIS

An important element in designing a STRATEGY; an analysis of the slowest elements that have to occur in sequence. The addition of the time taken to perform each of the elements in this sequence is the minimum time that it will take to implement the whole strategy.

Critical path analysis applies to all aspects of strategy such as new product introductions and R&D. However, it is most frequently used in large manufacturing or construction projects. While some phases of a project can be done simultaneously, others must be completed sequentially. These sequential tasks establish the critical path. It is especially important to identify lead times for purchased equipment and potential bottlenecks in the critical path in order to avoid unexpected delays in the project.

### CROSS-BORDER ALLIANCE

A strategic alternative to acquisition: a union formed with another firm interested in the same business area. As companies spread across the globe, more and more preferred cross-border alliances to setting up GREENFIELD SITES, making an acquisition, or signing a licensing agreement.

The management consultant firm MCKINSEY examined a number of cross-border alliances by large companies. It found that half were successful for both partners, and a third were successful for neither partner. This is about the same success rate as for cross-border acquisitions.

McKinsey went on to identify five characteristics common to cross-border alliances:

1.  Whereas acquisitions work well for core businesses and existing geographic areas, alliances are more effective when edging into related businesses or new geographic markets.

2. Alliances between strong and weak companies rarely work.

3. Successful alliances are distinguished by their ability to evolve beyond initial expectations and objectives.

4. Alliances with an even split of financial ownership are more likely to succeed than those in which one partner holds a majority interest. What matters is clear management control, not financial ownership.

5. More than three-quarters of the alliances that came to an end did so through an acquisition by one parent or the other.

**CROSS-BORDER TAKEOVER**

With the European Community's single-market program and the internationalization of all business, the volume and number of cross-border takeovers and acquisitions have increased dramatically. There are three unique dimensions to cross-border deals. They involve:

1. **Different legal systems.** In particular the contrast between Anglo-Saxon systems and Napoleonic-style systems found in continental Europe. Anglo-Saxon law is built on case histories, continental law on Napoleonic Code. Under Napoleonic systems citizens can do anything that is specifically allowed; under Anglo-Saxon systems they can do anything that is not specifically disallowed.

2. **Different capital markets.** Here there are two main cross-border differences, one related to the amount that companies raise from stock markets as opposed to other securities markets and banks, the other to the voting rights that go with different shares and

the control this can give to small groups of minority shareholders.

3. **Different cultures.** If this is not addressed by management with proper training, it can derail the most strategically exciting cross-border deal ever devised.

### CROSS-SUBSIDIZATION

The practice of selling one product at a loss in order to sell more of another at a profit. Consider razors and razor blades. Suppose (as has long been the case) that the profit margins are thin on razors but fat on blades. If a company can sell a lot of razors of a type that can take only its make of blade, then it is an excellent strategy to market the razors aggressively — even by selling them below cost — in order to sell (later) lots of profitable blades. Similarly, in the computer industry, as long as one manufacturer's products were not compatible with those of any other manufacturer, it made sense for companies to sell the initial hardware at cost price (or below) in order to tie customers into buying additional products in their range.

The danger with cross-subsidization is that it is a system of "give now, take later." A company may find that its industry has evolved in such a way that when it is time to take, the opportunity has disappeared. With computers, for example, any one manufacturer's models are increasingly compatible with any other's. Suppose in such a situation that a manufacturer has sold its basic PC at cost, and that by the time the customer is ready for add-ons, others are producing them at much lower margins. The manufacturer may find then that there is no profit in any part of its computer division. Likewise the razor manufacturer may find that a competitor (seeing the profit potential in razor blades) very quickly starts to manufacture blades that fit the original manufacturer's razor — and at a lower price.

## CROWN JEWELS

A defense against TAKEOVER in which a company sells its most precious assets to a friendly buyer. The suitor then disappears because the target of the pursuit has gone elsewhere, and the company rebuys its assets from its friend. (See also PAC-MAN DEFENSE, POISON PILL, SCORCHED-EARTH DEFENSE, SHARK REPELLANT)

---

*For business purposes the boundaries that separate one nation from another are no more real than the equator.*

Jacques Maisonrouge, IBM

---

## CSC/INDEX

Index was founded in 1969 by Tom Garrety, now dean of the Wharton School, and a group of colleagues from the Massachusetts Institute of Technology (MIT). The firm originally developed proprietary software for indexing stock portfolios (an indexed portfolio is a statistically selected mix of stocks that will move with the market), hence the name Index. That early work led to consulting on the strategic use of information technology, ultimately changing the firm's focus to BUSINESS PROCESS redesign. Working closely with consultant Michael Hammer, the firm pioneered the concept of REENGINEERING.

## CULTURE AUDIT

A systemic recording of all the factors that make up a company's culture. It is a useful way for companies to recognize that their CORPORATE CULTURE is not defined only by "hard" factors such as MISSION STATEMENTS and the company hierarchy; it is also determined by "soft" factors.

These soft factors have been classified by Gerry Johnson of the Cranfield Business School:

- **Rituals and routines.** For example, the need in some partnerships for everything that goes to clients to be signed by a partner.

- **Stories and myths.** Tales of legendary CEOs and of disastrous new products.

- **Symbols.** Special dining rooms for top executives or forms of address for the chief executive (e.g., "Sir" or "P.J."). This particular type of cultural factor is firmly eschewed by Japanese firms, perhaps because they have so many cultural symbols in their society that they do not need to create more inside the corporation.

---

*Culture is the collective programming of the mind which distinguishes the members of one human group from another.*

Geert Hofstede

## DAIMLER-BENZ

The largest German manufacturing company and one of the few major multinational groups that followed a strategy of **DIVERSIFICATION** in the 1980s, when most companies were being advised to "stick to their knitting." Daimler-Benz moved away from its **CORE COMPETENCE** in four-wheeled vehicles (it was the world's biggest manufacturer of trucks), and bought the ailing AEG domestic-appliance manufacturer. It then went into the aerospace industry, buying control of MBB (the M stands for Messerschmidt), Dornier, and MTU.

Daimler-Benz epitomizes the close relationship that German manufacturing companies have with their bankers. The **CHAIRMAN** of the supervisory **BOARD** (the nonexecutive tier of Germany's two-tier boards) is almost always ex-officio the chairman of **DEUTSCHE BANK**, the company's main banker.

*If we wish to be successful, we need quite simply a healthy mix of both familiar and progressive technologies, each contained in its own market-orientated division.*

*We are also aware that at the higher levels of management too we must resolutely aim for internationalization if we are to maintain our ground successfully in global competition.*

Edzard Reuter, chairman of Daimler-Benz's managing board

### Dawn raid

A colorful expression for the unexpected early-morning purchase on the stock market of a large block of shares by an investor who has an eye to taking over the company. This is aimed at preempting another potential raider from gaining a similar stranglehold on the TARGET of the TAKEOVER.

The expression has gained a new meaning in the 1990s, when nobody is taking over anything. It now refers to the raids on company premises carried out by EC officials intent on finding documentary evidence of collusion between companies in areas such as price fixing. Cement producers and chemical manufacturers have been popular targets. But EC officials don't do their raiding until long after dawn has broken.

### Decentralization

See CENTRALIZATION

### Declining industry

An industry whose market seems to be contracting inevitably and irreversibly — good examples are the markets for vinyl records and audio tapes. Declining industries present managers with a formidable question. What to do about the existing capacity in the market?

A classic MARKETING response is to "harvest" the product for all it's worth — raising prices, cutting advertising expenditure, and pruning product lines. Other companies choose to invest in promotion with an eye on obtaining LEADERSHIP in whatever is left of the market when (and if) it stops declining.

The STRATEGY to be followed depends largely on the company's view of the decline. Few declines are inevitable and predictable before they happen. Even fewer are smooth while they are happening. Strategy has to be determined partly by what rivals in the market are doing at the same time. If they are cutting CAPACITY rapidly in a bolt for the exit, then it may be prudent to aim for leadership of a shrunken market. If the BARRIER TO EXIT is high, however, it may be better to harvest what's left as fast as possible.

### DELAYERING

See FLAT ORGANIZATION

### DELEGATION

The process of transferring AUTHORITY from one person to another. Delegation once had connotations of "passing the buck," but it is now seen as a key part of the process of EMPOWERMENT.

### DELPHI TECHNIQUE

A technique for making decisions based on the ways of the ancient oracle at Delphi in Greece. The oracle was renowned for its impartiality, reaching decisions that warring parties were unable to make unaided.

The technique attempts to eliminate conflict between individual members of a group. A CHAIRMAN asks each member of the group for, say, an investment proposal in writing, considers all of them, and writes a short summary. The summary is then passed back to the members of the group, who are asked to submit revised proposals in consideration of the comments. This process is continued until consensus is reached. The Delphi technique has been used widely, and can work quite well even when members of the group are geographically disparate (especially so since the invention of the fax machine). But it is a slow process and relies heavily on the total impartiality of the chairman.

### DEUTSCHE BANK

Germany's mightiest financial institution, founded in Berlin in 1870. Its status today is symbolized by its two massive towers dominating the skyline of Frankfurt, the country's financial capital.

Deutsche Bank has an unmatched influence on German industry. It lends to it, owns large chunks of it, underwrites new equity issues, coordinates financial restructurings, advises its management (it owns the well-known management consultancy Roland Berger), and frequently provides its boards with nonexecutive directors.

Despite having branches and subsidiaries all over the world and publishing its annual report in German, Spanish, French, English, and Japanese, Deutsche Bank remains a very German institution. Its powerful management committee (which traditionally acts as a single unit with a "spokesman," not a CHAIRMAN) is entirely German. The bank's recent efforts have been concentrated on expanding into eastern Germany where it has its roots.

### DIFFERENTIATION

The process of identifying the positive way in which a company's product differs from its rivals and using this as the basis for charging a premium price. BRANDING creates customer loyalty through advertising and promotion.

New tastes and fashions provide all sorts of opportunities for differentiation. In recent years, developments such as the interest in health foods and concern for the environment have given companies opportunities to differentiate their products as "containing more fiber" or being "environmentally more friendly" than existing products.

PEPSICO spent fortunes advertising the fact that in "blind" tests three people out of every five preferred the taste of Pepsi to that of Coke. (There really is a difference — Pepsi is sweeter.) Yet more people continued to buy Coke than Pepsi, in part because they were not just buying taste. Above all they were buying a statement about themselves. Even if the products tasted exactly the same, they preferred Coke because it differentiated them.

Additional features, additional service, and even a higher price are common sources of differentiation.

### DIRECTOR

Company directors come in two varieties: executive and nonexecutive. In countries such as Germany and Sweden the two are separated — the executive directors sit on the management board, and the nonexecutives sit on the supervisory board. From there they keep an eye on the management board, deciding grandly on things like who is to be CEO, and how much top executives should be paid.

In Anglo-Saxon economies, executives and nonexecutives sit together around the same table. In these unitary boards there is a tendency for responsibility for particular functions to be delegated to relevant subcommittees. For example, almost all American boards have subcommittees to consider the questions of executive directors' remuneration, auditing, and the appointment of auditors. These subcommittees usually consist of a subset of the nonexecutive directors.

Nonexecutive directors are usually chosen from the circle of the **CHAIRMAN**'s acquaintances. In the United States they are often the chief executives of other companies, whereas many U.K. boardrooms still echo with the influence of public schools and Oxford and Cambridge.

On the one hand, this may be a good thing — groups of like-minded people are apt to work comfortably together. On the other hand, a bunch of like-minded people is not likely to foster dissent when dissent is needed (as it often is). (See also **BOARD** and **CHAIRMAN**)

## DISCLOSURE

The disclosure of information by companies is a source of constant tension. Various authorities (government, for example) demand it, and so does the general public (as consumers, and also increasingly as sharers of the same environment). Yet given the choice, most companies would prefer not to reveal information — not because they are up to no good, but because of the **COMPETITIVE ADVANTAGE** that information gives to their rivals. At least for as long as their rivals are publishing as much information as they are, the game is being played on a level playing field. (See **INSIDE INFORMATION**)

Certain disclosure requirements are obligatory.

- All companies have to file annual financial statements — in the majority of cases an income statement and a balance sheet, and increasingly a flow-of-funds statement.

- In most countries publicly traded companies have to file further information with stock exchange authorities when they want to raise money on the capital markets. In the United States the authority is the SEC (the Securities and Exchange Commission). For many companies — foreign ones in particular — the disclosure requirements of the SEC are a serious deterrent to obtaining a listing on the New York Stock Exchange. The cost of producing the information required can be truly prohibitive.

- In the United States quarterly financial reports are required and closely scrutinized by investors. Critics blame these quarterly reporting requirements for the short-term financial orientation of many U.S. companies. (See **INSIDE INFORMATION**)

## DISTRIBUTION MIX

The combination of channels that a company uses to distribute its products from the factory gate to the marketplace. Distribution mix will be a combination of the following channels:

- Very direct, as with those companies that have a shop on their factory site (common with glass or ceramic manufacturers)
- Slightly less direct, as through the mail straight from factory to the customer (called direct mail)
- Straight to traditional retail outlets
- Through one or more wholesalers to traditional retail outlets

The profitability of selling through these different channels will be different and will change over time. Companies need to be sure, therefore, that (less profit-

able) sales through a string of wholesalers are not de-
tracting from potentially greater sales through direct
mail. (See also CHANNEL OF DISTRIBUTION)

---

*Distributors who do not make commitments
to use technology available to them today
may not be in business in 1995. That
technology includes laser scanning,
state-of-the-art bar coding, and
on-line direct order entry.*

From an Arthur Andersen study:
"The Technology Maze in Wholesale Distribution"

---

### DIVERSIFICATION

A popular STRATEGY in the 1960s and 1970s when companies went into any business that took their fancy. The
impetus behind this was an emphasis on financial management and earnings-per-share growth as primary
strategic objectives. This created oil companies in electronics and tobacco companies in insurance. Many di-
versifications ended up in tears, and as a strategy it has
been replaced by an emphasis on staying within one's
field. Nevertheless, there are still opportunities for
profitable diversification — but only where the benefits
from shared activities can be clearly foreseen and easily
quantified.

### DIVESTMENT

The opposite of acquisition — the disposal of a business
either by selling it off or by closing it down. A divest-

ment requires as much thought and planning as an acquisition, including careful consideration of timing (should the business be sold or can it be successfully harvested?), **BARRIERS TO EXIT**, and potential buyers. A business that is unprofitable for the seller may be very attractive to another company with a different strategy or mix of business.

### DIVIDEND POLICY

A major decision for the **BOARD** of any public company is what dividend to pay its shareholders. In many cases shareholders have become like creditors, expecting dividends at least at the same level as last year, regardless of the company's performance. Maintaining a dividend has drained many companies of cash at a time when they are in dire need of it; and the thought of having to maintain it in the future has made many companies keep their dividend down when they could have increased it. In short, too many shareholders have strayed away from their original purpose as the providers of risk capital, and have turned into quasi-moneylenders.

There are some notable exceptions to this: **MICRO-SOFT**, the world's leading software firm, has never paid a dividend since it went public in 1986; and Japanese companies are notorious for their ungenerous dividend policies.

### DOMINANT POSITION

Article 86 of the Treaty of Rome, which set up the European Community, prevents companies in the community from abusing "a dominant position." That is just about all the treaty has to say about the crucial areas of competition policy, monopolies, and mergers — crucial areas for Europe's rapidly integrating industries.

In a landmark ruling in 1973, in a case involving Continental Can, the European Court decreed that Article 86 can be used to block mergers if they leave matters such that "the only undertakings in the market are those which are dependent on the dominant undertaking with regard to their market behavior."

At the end of the 1980s, the EC Commission got greater direct powers to examine mergers and indeed to unscramble them if they are, in its view, anticompetitive. Since then there has been no large TAKEOVER in Europe without prior discussion with Brussels. (See also OLIGOPOLY)

### DOWNSIZING

Global competition and the restructuring of many industries require a "leaner and meaner" organization. Bloated corporations achieve this by downsizing. In theory, the organization becomes more efficient as unnecessary positions are eliminated. In fact, the supposedly lucky survivors of downsizing often assume significant responsibilities of former colleagues and morale problems begin to interfere with productivity.

### DOWNSTREAM

A concept that has become more vivid since Michael Porter and others made us think of companies as a series of links in a chain (see VALUE CHAIN). All manufacturing of goods and provision of services can be seen as a series of links — from digging up raw materials to adding bar codes to product packaging.

In an analogy with rivers, those links near the source

of the operation (e.g., digging up raw materials) are said to be "upstream"; those links near the mouth of the river (that is, close to the ocean of consumers) are said to be "downstream."

Companies can then be defined as having a "center of gravity" that is either upstream or downstream. Oil companies are the classic example of upstream businesses that attempt to move downstream: first by refining oil into other oil products, then by moving into the manufacture of petrochemicals. Most companies seeking to diversify look first just upstream or just downstream of their centers of gravity.

Recently companies have allied with downstream or upstream businesses in an effort to compete more efficiently.

### DREXEL BURNHAM LAMBERT

The brokerage firm that almost single-handedly invented the junk bond market in the 1980s. The market was developed and manipulated by Michael Milken, a shy mathematical gymnast who ran the market out of the company's Los Angeles office. By the end of the decade Drexel had gone bust, and Michael Milken had gone to jail.

They had also succeeded in giving junk a bad name. Drexel's original purpose was to enable a wider range of American companies to have access to the corporate bond market. Only those (few) with a satisfactory rating from the duopoly of credit-rating agencies had access to the market. Drexel and Milken persuaded investors that the extra return on bonds without a suitable rating (i.e., junk) was worth the extra RISK.

Problems arose because the market failed to distinguish properly between those junk bonds that did not have a rating because they were too small, too new, or too remote, and those that did not have a rating because of their deteriorating financial position (true junk).

## DUMPING

The process of selling goods in a foreign market at prices that are below cost or below the price for which they are being sold in their domestic market. Such activity is unpopular in most places and illegal in some. It is usually assumed to be something that Far Eastern manufacturers do to European and American markets. But the Koreans have accused the French of dumping cement in their market, and the Koreans in turn have been accused by the Japanese of dumping textiles. (See also ANTIDUMPING)

## Earnings Per Share (EPS)

A ubiquitous yardstick of a company's performance — its total earnings (profit) divided by the number of its shares. This provides a comparison with previous years for the same company; in order to compare one company's performance with another company's, the measuring rod has to be the P/E ratio, which relates EPS to a company's share price. For some companies the relentless pursuit of growth in earnings per share has become an overriding goal. In these companies long-term strategic objectives are sacrificed to quarterly and year-end financial reports.

Such ratios are unsatisfactory as measures of performance for at least two reasons.

1. They take no account of a company's future prospects; the company that plows back much of its profit into research will have a lower EPS than one that does not, but few investors are willing or able to take this into account.

2. They take no account of benefits accruing to interested parties other than shareholders. The company that pays its managers well will have a lower EPS than the company that pays them badly (assuming it stops short of paying peanuts and getting monkeys).

In consequence, countries that pay most attention to EPS (and to P/E ratios) are those, like America and Britain, that have an exceptionally short-term business outlook and an excessive concern for shareholders' interests.

## ECONOMIES OF SCALE

One of the most fundamental ideas in the economics of the firm, and one of the most misunderstood — the idea that the larger the quantity of a product or service that is produced, the lower the average cost per unit.

This occurs because fixed costs can be spread more widely. Thus a given amount of advertising can be spread more thinly (in terms of cost per unit) over a product of which 10 $x$ are sold than over a product of which only $x$ are sold. Economies of scale also arise from the fact that some (efficient) technologies can only be applied above a certain production level — large transport systems, for example, or continuous production lines. (See also BARRIER TO ENTRY)

If economies of scale can be applied ad infinitum, then all firms would aim to grow indefinitely. But they have their limits — above a certain size, diseconomies of scale begin to set in: the sheer cost of managing so many people and so much equipment begins to offset the advantages of adding yet another production line, and so forth. These diseconomies are sometimes called the costs of complexity.

The technology of certain industries (for instance, steel where small-scale furnaces can now produce specialty steels economically in low volumes) has destroyed any blind assumption that economies of scale are always beneficial.


## ECONOMIES OF SCOPE

This is a somewhat different concept from ECONOMIES OF SCALE. It is savings in unit cost from producing or supplying a range of products (as opposed to a larger quantity of the same product). The savings here come in distribution, R&D, and central services such as accounting and **PUBLIC RELATIONS**.

Economies of scope often underlie the reasons given for diversification strategies. Japanese electronics companies such as Hitachi and **MATSUSHITA** manufacture photocopiers, fax machines, telephones, printers, and personal computers because all these products are aimed at the same market: the market for office equipment.

### EMERGENT INDUSTRY

Steering a young growing company in a young growing (e.g., emergent) industry requires special skills. Some of the particular problems to be faced:

- Uncertainty as to the eventual market size
- Uncertainty as to the eventual product configuration
- Shortage of special skills needed for the industry
- The absence of widely agreed-on standards
- Lack of faith in the long-term viability of the industry among suppliers, investors, bankers, and so forth

In *The Strategy Handbook*, Michael Hay and Peter Williamson, two academics at the London Business School, list the following general rules for companies in emergent industries.

- Place low-cost bets on alternative technologies early on through the use of cross-licensing.
- Seek out a few sophisticated launch customers that can act as opinion leaders. Focus on them, even at little profit, rather than seeking to broaden the customer base too quickly.
- Get market reactions to a product quickly; don't wait too long trying to perfect it.

- Invest in the development of product technology, in the required process technology, and in the support products, all in parallel. Don't wait until the product is complete before sorting out the problems of how to manufacture it or how to supply users with essential support services.

- Recognize changes in the basis of COMPETITION as quickly as possible, for in such an industry such changes will be frequent.

- Look toward the END GAME — when the industry will have settled down — to see how profit can be maximized at that time, rather than in the uncertain turmoil that will lead up to it in an emergent industry.

### EMPLOYEE INVOLVEMENT (EI)

Teamwork, when it includes nonmanagers, becomes employee involvement. Quality improvement programs frequently include EI. Not surprisingly, employees often have good suggestions to make about QUALITY.

### EMPLOYEE PARTICIPATION

A general term for ways in which employees can participate more fully in the running of the company. These range from the "idea box" popular with some Japanese companies, to the loan schemes run by some companies in the West to enable employees to buy their company's shares. (See also CO-DETERMINATION)

### EMPOWERMENT

The process of moving power, information, and rewards downward in the organization. Empowering people literally gives them the power to do something, and as a result they become more responsible and cooperative.

Edward E. Lawler III, of the University of Southern California's Center for Effective Organizations, believes that empowerment requires that "you create small business units, you flatten the organization, you change work systems and design, and you change the role of the manager" (*Business Week*, August 31, 1992, p. 49). It is extremely difficult for management to give up AU-THORITY and for employees to translate newly found power into increased productivity (see also EMPLOYEE INVOLVEMENT, SELF-MANAGED TEAMS)

## END GAME

The STRATEGY for the final days of a company, a product, or a business unit. Basically, it involves deciding between whether to

- bleed the product for all it's worth before it dies a natural death,
- try to steer it into a comfortable little niche where it can continue to be a nice little earner for some time to come, or
- encourage the COMPETITION to close (by an aggressive pricing policy, for example) in the hope of securing a large share of what little market can be kindled after its disappearance. (See also DECLINING INDUSTRY)

## ENVIRONMENTAL AUDIT

A method of ensuring that systems that minimize a company's adverse impact on the environment are actually in place and working, and that the company is continually complying with environmental legislation. First introduced in the early 1970s, mostly by companies in the chemical and petrochemicals industries, environmental audits grew in popularity after Union Carbide's fatal leak at Bhopal in the mid-1980s.

Large companies in environmentally sensitive businesses (like **ROYAL DUTCH/SHELL** and **BP**) have carried out environmental audits for some years. At Shell teams of three to five people examine sites about once a year. Their work is confidential and internal (non-Shell employees are not involved). Many companies, however, bring in outside consultants for their environmental audits. BP widens its audit to look at a different "issue" each year. In 1990, it looked at its impact on wetlands.

### Equity method

A method of accounting for companies in which the owner has a significant stake, but not control. A significant stake is usually defined as something between 20% and 50%, but the equity method may be used (instead of consolidation) when the stake is over 50% if the **STAKEHOLDER** does not thereby control the company's activities. It can also be used if the stake is less than 20% but is enough to give the stakeholder significant influence over the company's activities. (For example, if voting rights are out of proportion to ownership.)

Under the equity method the investor includes in its profits a percentage (in line with its stake) of the company's profits, regardless of whether they are distributed as dividends or not. These profits have already been taxed, so for the investor they amount to a tax-free addition to the bottom line. That may look good in the inspector's financial statements, but it does not represent a single extra "real" dollar in its coffers.

## ETHICS

The vexing question of what is right and wrong in everyday behavior. Business ethics are the codes of behavior over and above which professionals and businesspeople agree among themselves constitute the proper way to deal with the general public, and with one another.

Ethics are particularly important in professions such as law, medicine, and the media. Some companies (DuPont is one) have formalized ethical codes that articulate their responsibilities to various **STAKEHOLDERS**. One of the most prevalent ethical problems is conflicting standards of behavior in different national cultures, such as payment to government officials in government contracts.

## EXCELLENCE

A cult created by Tom Peters and Robert Waterman in their blockbusting best-seller, *In Search of Excellence*. First published in 1982, the book was a search for companies in America that could still be described as "excellent" despite a popular belief at the time that soon only Japanese industry would be able to produce **QUALITY**.

Tom Peters started his later book, *Thriving on Chaos*, by stating that there are no excellent companies.

## EXCESS CAPACITY

See **CAPACITY**

## EXIT ROUTE

The way by which an investor (especially a venture capitalist) is eventually to realize the gain on an investment. For example, will the company go public, thereby enabling him or her to sell shares on the stock market? Or will there be a sale for cash to a larger group? Sometimes it appears unseemly to hear so much talk of exit routes before anything has been entered into. (See also **BARRIER TO EXIT**)

### EXPERIENCE CURVE

A dominant influence on competitive position, particularly in high-tech industries, an experience curve causes unit costs to decline as cumulative production increases. This happens because workers become more proficient at their jobs, manufacturing processes are improved, and support services begin to function smoothly. As a result, according to the theory, the competitor that expands production capacity fastest will achieve a cost advantage that leads to industry dominance, hence the popularity of cost-based strategies. Relentless pursuit of cost leadership, however, can lead a company to ignore other important dimensions of competition such as **QUALITY** and service.

First observed in manufacturing industries as the "learning curve," the concept was broadened beyond the assembly line and applied to strategy by Bruce Henderson, founder of **THE BOSTON CONSULTING GROUP**. It fueled that firm's phenomenal growth in the 1970s.

### EXPONENTIAL SMOOTHING

A technique for forecasting in which a weighted average of past data is used as the basis for a forecast. Recent readings are given greater weight than those from further in the past on the grounds that recent events are more relevant to future performance than are long-ago ones.

## EXTERNALITIES

The incidental effects on others of one person's or one company's behavior. These effects may be beneficial (when somebody's newly painted house enhances the whole neighborhood) or they may be damaging (when McDonald's customers discard their litter in the streets surrounding the restaurant).

The issue about externalities is this: Who pays for them? The whole neighborhood does not make a contribution toward the one cleanly painted house in its midst.

Concern about industrial destruction of the environment has brought the issue of externalities more into the corporate arena. Who is to pay for cleaning our rivers? Many countries pay lip service to the principle that the polluter pays. But the small fines imposed on the guilty in most cases show how ineffective this can be in practice. (EXXON, as you shall see, is a notable exception.)

## EXXON

The former Standard Oil Company of New Jersey, forced to change its trade name from Esso (the "so" stood for Standard Oil) by other Standard Oil companies, spent $100 million on finding Exxon. A computer threw out the name, which was then checked against hundreds of dictionaries to ensure that it was meaningless and without significance in most of the languages that humanity has created.

Like many of its fellow oil giants, Exxon has gone in for more than a drop of DIVERSIFICATION. It is one of America's largest chemical companies and has large interests in coal. It owns a copper mine in Chile and had a brief but fruitless foray into high-technology optoelectronics in the late 1970s.

The company had to learn about CRISIS MANAGEMENT when one of its tankers (the *Exxon Valdez*) ran aground in Alaska in 1989. The 11 million gallons of oil that spewed along the coast was the most costly environmental mistake a company has ever had to pay for. In a court settlement in 1991 Exxon agreed to hand over $1.15 billion toward the cost of the cleanup.

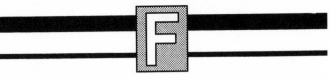

## FACTOR ANALYSIS

A statistical procedure in which a number of variables (quantities that vary) are reduced by finding clusters of variables (called factors) that are interrelated. For example, football players can be differentiated by a number of variables: height, muscular build, agility, speed, intelligence, sight, and so forth. All this information can be categorized under two factors: mental and physical.

## FACTORING

The practice of selling a company's debts to another company (the factoring company) at a discount (which can be as much as 5%). The factoring company then collects the debts and hopes to retrieve more than it paid for them. The advantage for the company selling its debts in this way is that it improves CASH FLOW. The disadvantage is that customers may think that the company has resorted to factoring because it is in financial difficulty. This latter problem can be bypassed by invoice discounting.

## FACTORS OF PRODUCTION

In the framework of classical economics there were traditionally three factors of production: land, labor, and capital. (Modern theory sometimes adds a fourth: entrepreneurship.) Goods and services are produced (and wealth created) by combining these factors in different proportions. For example, today steel production requires some land, little labor, and a lot of capital. Information processing requires little land, lots of labor, and little capital.

In some industries these proportions have changed over time. Farming, for example, used to require much land, little capital, and much labor. Now it requires less land, rather more capital, and much less labor.

The cost of these factors is

- rent (for land),
- interest (for capital), and
- wages and salaries (for labor).

## FAMILY FIRM

The family-owned business presents special management problems — not least of them those of succession and of board membership. IMD, a management school in Switzerland that runs special courses on the problems of the family firm, recounts the (true) story of the family father who would hand over the reins only on condition that his son speak five languages fluently and have a university degree. In another case an irate son removed his father from the head of the family business at gunpoint.

IMD claims that family businesses account for some 70% to 80% of all businesses worldwide. They account for significantly less of business turnover, although as a group they can be said to include such giants as Fiat, Hanson, Mars, and TOYOTA.

IMD had also found that 68% of family businesses fail in the first generation, 16% are sold or split up, and only 16% carry on to the next generation.

*Murder is commonly a family affair, as are numerous other unspeakable crimes that human beings perpetrate against each other. Any small business owner employing other people needs to bear this in mind. The more a business can boast that it is "just like a family" as far as relations between bosses and workers are concerned, the louder the alarm bells probably ought to ring.*

*Financial Times,* 1992

### FEEDBACK

As important in interpersonal contact as it is in systems design. Without feedback from fellow workers, an employee will be demotivated and wither. That was one of the principal findings of the famous Hawthorne experiments conducted at the General Electric factory near Chicago in the 1930s. Increasing (or decreasing) the lighting was enough feedback to motivate the Hawthorne workers. Conversely, when employees have an opportunity to give feedback to management, QUALITY and morale improve.

### FIELD THEORY

A psychological theory associated with Kurt Lewin that attempts to explain human motivation in terms of the environment in which a person operates, and not in terms solely of an individual's personality. As with a magnet, a "field" of forces bears on the individual and molds his or her behavior.

This has important implications for the workplace. It suggests that employees' performance can be changed as much by the ethos of the place in which they work as by their own individual financial incentives — that is, that a **MISSION STATEMENT** can improve performance as much as a pay increase.

## FINANCIAL ENGINEERING

This refers to a whole range of techniques used to juggle around with a company's balance sheet (or at least with the liabilities side of it). Sale-and-leaseback property deals are one example.

Financial engineering comes into its own when companies take each other over. Indeed, many a **TAKEOVER** in the 1980s seemed to be motivated by little other than a desire to indulge in it. For example, brand names can be valued on the balance sheet when they have been bought, but not when they have been built up from scratch. So a value of several hundred million dollars for the name Smirnoff suddenly appeared on the balance sheet of the hotel group Grand Metropolitan after it had bought the famous vodka.

---

*It is a truism that confidence is important to banks. That is why the early Hebrews did their banking in temples and the later Americans and Europeans built banks that looked like temples.*

The Wall Street Journal, 1992

---

## FLAT ORGANIZATION

The elimination of middle management, the product of **DOWNSIZING, EMPLOYEE INVOLVEMENT, REENGINEERING,** and a desire to make an organization more customer-oriented have resulted in the flat organization. Thanks to high-powered information systems and communications technology, the corporate ladder has fewer rungs.

The process of flattening organizations in this way is called DELAYERING.

In flat organizations the pecking order changes. In traditional hierarchical organizations AUTHORITY moves in one direction only and never changes. In the flat organization it can move in many directions, and it changes according to the task or project in hand.

### FLEXIBLE ORGANIZATION

"Flexible" has become one of management's favorite words. There are flexible manufacturing systems, in which computers and robots enable previously mass-produced items to be personalized; there is flextime, which allows employees to work at hours of their own choosing (around a central midday core); and above all, there are flexible organizations, in which nothing is so rigid that it cannot be changed at very short notice to meet a shift in market demand. This is a useful tool in the management of CHANGE.

### FOCUSING

A STRATEGY for achieving competitive advantage by dominating an important MARKET SEGMENT. Instead of trying to compete on cost or through DIFFERENTIATION, the focused competitor zeroes in on a market segment such as service that has distinct needs and focuses its efforts on serving these needs better than other competitors do. The focused competitor gives up a broadly based market and hopes to have picked a segment that will remain robust and distinct from other market segments.

## FOLLOWERS

In theory, many companies are faced with the strategic decision of whether to be a leader in their market or a follower. In practice, most companies set out to be leaders and end up by default as followers.

The real strategic issue is whether a leader can establish a market presence of sufficient strength to counterbalance the higher R&D and the bigger promotion costs involved in being first. The answer is probably "no" more often than most companies care to admit. The follower will always have the advantages of learning from the leader's mistakes and riding the coattails of the leader's efforts to develop a market. Many large companies hold back, letting smaller, more flexible rivals pioneer new markets. This has a certain merit. Pioneers of the American West sometimes ended up with arrows in their backs.

## FOREIGN DIRECT INVESTMENT (FDI)

The value of those substantial stakes in a nation's industry owned by foreigners. FDI does not include casual investments in a country's stocks and shares: those are known as portfolio investments. "Substantial" is usually something over 10% and an investment that the investor intends to hold for some time.

FDI is usually measured both as a "flow" figure and a "stock" figure. The flow figure shows the amount of net new investment in a period (the incoming investment less the outgoing investment); the stock figure indicates the cumulative value of all such investment at a particular point in time. The largest net new investors abroad are currently the Japanese, but they do not have the largest stock of FDI. That honor is reserved for the United States, followed by the United Kingdom.

In some senses, FDI is a substitute for trade. If country X is prevented from exporting to country Y (or it no longer makes economic sense for it to do so — because, perhaps, its wage costs have risen to prohibitive heights), then it can still penetrate country Y's market by investing in the country and manufacturing its products there (as the Japanese have done in Europe and America).

In recent years FDI has been growing far faster than trade. Where trade used to be the focus for international commercial disputes, FDI is increasingly taking over. The world will soon need a GATT for FDI. (See also MULTINATIONAL)

---

*America has invaded Europe not with armed men, but with manufactured goods. Its leaders have been captains of industry and skilled financiers whose conquests are having a profound effect on the lives of the masses from Madrid to St. Petersburg. Our aristocracy marry American wives, and their coachmen are giving place to American-trained drivers of American-built automobiles . . . our babies are fed on American foods, and our dead are buried in American coffins.*

from *The American Invaders*
by F. A. McKenzie, published in 1902

## FOREIGN EXCHANGE

The management of a company's foreign-exchange position can make (or lose) the company millions of dollars a year. Because foreign exchange markets (spot and forward) can be so volatile, it has always been a temptation for ambitious managers to take a gamble in them, especially when sagging mainstream earnings are in need of a boost. But the risks involved in such a gamble are terribly high. As has been proved time and time again, nobody can predict the way foreign exchange rates are going to move.

The European Monetary System and its Exchange Rate Mechanism (ERM) were one attempt to make foreign-exchange markets less volatile. The mechanism allows currencies of EC member-states to move only within a narrow band against one another. But it has been difficult to maintain the mechanism in the face of determined speculators and the giant waves of capital that are now free to swish around the world's major financial centers in search of short-term returns.

An increasingly pressing problem has arisen over the best way to translate foreign currency items in a company's accounts. There is no standard approved way of doing this, and several issues are in the air:

- What exchange rate should be used?
- How should gains or losses on conversion be treated in the accounts?
- What should be done about inflation in the country issuing the currency?

## FRANCHISING

Franchising offers a means for the successful manufacturer of a product, or the creator of a business system, to grow very quickly, freed from many of the chains imposed by limited capital resources. The franchiser shifts most of the initial setup costs of a retailing or wholesaling operation to the franchisee, and also collects a fee — anything up to 40%. In return, the franchisee gets to feel like an entrepreneur while selling a well-known brand name.

A vast range of goods have been (and still are) sold by franchise. These include such well-known names as Benetton and McDonald's as well as lesser-known (and highly successful) products and services such as hotel magazines. Franchises have been found to experience a lower failure rate than new businesses in general, and in some countries (e.g., Canada) now account for over 40% of all retail sales.

Despite its recent growth in popularity, franchising has a long lineage that can be traced back as far as medieval rulers who gave their subjects franchises to collect taxes in a particular geographical region. In return, the franchised subjects were allowed to keep a certain percentage of the taxes they collected. For these rulers, the strategic question was whether, as the franchiser, they were prepared to relinquish some control in return for greater geographical scope and, they hoped, greater returns.

#### FUNCTIONAL STRUCTURE

The organization of a company according to function. For example: marketing, accounts, production, human resources. This classic form of corporate structure, often called the unitary structure, is the first and obvious choice for almost every small and new company. But it has its limitations.

As companies grow, each functional department tends to get isolated and defensive about its territory, passing off awkward responsibilities ("You'll have to ask accounts") and clinging anxiously to privileges. In some cases, such as the legal and accounting departments, professional identity further exacerbates the problem of conflicting loyalties endemic in the functional structure. Yet the purpose of the corporation is to have all functions working together. No company can consist solely of an accounting department.

A growing realization of the need for cross-functional integration — for the accounting department to talk more to the production people, and for the R&D department to talk to the marketing experts, for example — has led many companies to rethink their functional structure.

There is a new emphasis on customer orientation that exhorts each function to look on all of its end-users, internal as well as external, as "customers" and to treat them accordingly. When companies become involved in REENGINEERING, they look beyond the functional structure to determine which tasks relate to critical business processes rather than group tasks by function.

## FUNDS-FLOW ANALYSIS

This consists of a detailed examination of the sources and timing of the funds that flow into a company and the funds that flow out of it. Such funds include cash from sales or cash spent on the purchase of raw materials. They also include the value of goods bought or sold on credit.

Such analysis can reveal details about the average terms of credit given and received. Small changes in these terms and conditions of payment may make a considerable difference to a company's working capital and to its capacity to operate profitably.

## GAME THEORY

The theory that business bears much resemblance to games in the sense that a move by one player sparks off moves by others. Game theory formalizes the study of problems where any move depends on the moves of others — and on the correct or incorrect anticipation of the moves of others. This is particularly relevant to concentrated industries. The language of games pervades the language of business — "level playing-field," "zero sum game." (See also **END GAME**)

The most appropriate game for the businessperson to study is probably chess; there have been notable businesspeople who have been adept chess players. It does not work the other way around, however. Brilliant chess player that he is, Bobby Fischer is not a great businessman.

## GANTT CHARTS

Named after Henry L. Gantt, these were for many decades management's principal planning tool. Developed in 1917 and 1918 to help plan wartime production, they involved plotting time along one scale and different tasks along the other. Each task was then represented by a solid bar that stretched across the time it took to be performed.

Such simplistic diagrams may still be helpful in production planning and control. But with the increasing computerization of the planning process they have become largely redundant.

## GENERAL ELECTRIC (GE)

Like other large, well-established U.S. companies, General Electric discovered early that "business as usual" would not be enough to meet the challenge of lean, highly productive global competitors. General Electric is the company where strategic planning began; GE pioneered the concept of the STRATEGIC BUSINESS UNIT, analyzed its SBUs by means of a BUSINESS ATTRACTIVENESS/INDUSTRY STRENGTH MATRIX, and used data about their performance for the development of the PIMS program. Today GE is rushing to simplify, to reduce its bureaucracy and the resulting complicated decision-making process in order to respond more quickly to changing markets.

The process began in 1981, when John F. Welch, Jr., became GE's chairman and CEO. He embarked on a redirection of the company that would focus its operations on three "strategic circles": core manufacturing units such as lighting and locomotives, technology-intensive businesses, and services. Welch's objective was for each business to be first or second in the global marketplace; this objective has been achieved by slashing costs, increasing productivity, and improving quality.

Welch has now turned his attention to changing the attitudes and motivation levels of his employees. Convinced that the leaner GE needs empowered employees, he is leading an effort to identify and eliminate unproductive work and believes it unrealistic to expect employees in a leaner organization to complete the paperwork that was once standard procedure. Welch is also trying to instill a sense of ownership and commitment in his employees. He is hoping to inspire improved performance and stimulate suggestions for change that will

further improve performance. This motivational program he calls "Work-Out."

*Incremental change doesn't work very well
in the type of transformation GE is going
through. If your change isn't big enough,
revolutionary enough, the bureaucracy can
beat you. When you get leaders who confuse
popularity with leadership, who just nibble
away at things, nothing changes.*

Jack Welch, in Noel M. Tichy and Stratford Sherman,
*Control Your Destiny or Someone Else Will: How Jack
Welch Is Making General Electric the World's Most
Competitive Company* (Doubleday/Currency, 1993)

### GENERAL MOTORS

The biggest American car company, and for many years
the biggest private manufacturing company in the
world, with sales greater than the GNP of an entire
small country such as Sweden. Along with the other
American car companies, it has lurched like a yo-yo in
recent years — profits of $4.86 billion in 1988 were
counterbalanced by losses of $4.45 billion in 1991.

That was enough to move the company's nonexecutive directors (spurred on by its institutional shareholders) to throw out the CHIEF EXECUTIVE OFFICER in a rare
instance of owners dictating to top management in a
way other than by TAKEOVER (see also BP).

As part of its recovery from a disastrous 1991, the

company planned "a reduction of executive compensation." It also made no annual incentive awards to its employees.

---

*Revitalizing General Motors is like teaching an elephant to tap dance. You find the sensitive spots and start poking.*

H. Ross Perot, once on GM's board

---

### GENERIC STRATEGY

In his classic book, *Competitive Strategy*, Michael Porter identifies three separate classes of strategy as vehicles for competitive advantage. These are cost leadership (see COST LEADER), DIFFERENTIATION, and FOCUSING. A company that does not follow one of these strategies is "stuck in the middle" and vulnerable to competitors. The clever strategist will figure out which strategy will apply to a specific industry — or better yet, rewrite the rules of the industry to implement one of those options.

### GIGO

Garbage In, Garbage Out — one of many business expressions that started with a specialist computer application and came to have wider significance (others include networking and interface). GIGO began as an expression about computer data — the truism that if you put data that are garbage into a computer, then the only thing you can hope to get out of it will also be garbage. But it has been expanded with a twist to apply to management.

## GLOBAL FIRM

A firm that is organized and managed to take advantage of whatever synergies are available across country markets. The global firm sells and may also manufacture in many countries. It sells, however, a standardized product, perhaps also standardizing brand name, positioning, and advertising content. It manufactures at whatever sites will minimize delivered cost across its country markets. Although there is no single best model, the global firm organizes itself in a way that facilitates efficient marketing, manufacture, and distribution worldwide.

*For Toyota, becoming a global company has meant becoming a local company in scores of nations: cultivating business opportunity as a member of local industry: and shouldering social responsibility as a member of the community.*

Toyota Annual Report

## GLOBAL INDUSTRY

A global industry is one where a firm's activities in one country market can affect its competitive position in other country markets.

*Global localization.*

A Sony slogan

## GOLDMAN SACHS

The investment bank that, perhaps, best kept its head in the 1980s when all about it were losing theirs (see SALOMON BROTHERS). Its high reputation goes back to the 1950s when it was chosen to advise the Ford family on taking their car company public. It is known for refusing to work with companies intending to make hostile takeovers.

Despite making profits of $600 million in 1990, Goldman Sachs was not wholly uninfluenced by the gloom on Wall Street. Like all its rivals, it cut both costs and jobs.

## GOODWILL

The amount by which the price of a business (bought as a going concern) exceeds the value of all its assets. This can be seen as the capitalized value of the extra profits that the company will earn because it is not a newly formed company with the same assets.

Goodwill is the sum of several intangible assets that are not embedded in the shop floor. These include things like brand loyalty, efficient systems, CORPORATE CULTURE, and know-how. Accountants have great difficulty in deciding how to account for goodwill. Differences in common practice between the United Kingdom and the United States are said to show U.K. companies in a better light than their U.S. rivals, to their COMPETITIVE ADVANTAGE.

## GOVERNANCE

A hot issue for the 1990s, alternatively defined by the Swiss business school IMD, as

*a question of performance accountability . . . the
various legal frameworks for corporate activity ultimately deal with the questions: to whom, and for
what, corporations shall be held accountable.*

Interest in governance arose partly from a feeling that
companies were being run too much in the interests of
either their managers or their shareholders. Other stakeholders in the company were being ignored.

- Marketers emphasized the significance of the customer and of being a customer-led corporation.
- Information technology put the emphasis on the employee; the value of the corporation lay in his or her
  head, not in arms and legs.
- The general public, aware of the environmental damage caused by corporations, demanded that the environment come high up on the corporate agenda.

The right balance to strike between these frequently
competing demands had to be decided in the boardroom.
That turned the focus of the debate about governance
onto questions of how to construct more effective
boards. (See also **BOARD**, **DIRECTOR**, and **STAKEHOLDER**)

### GREENFIELD SITE

A field (or two), usually on the outskirts of an old town,
on which a company can build a factory, warehouse, or
other sort of plant. When deciding where to locate new
plant, a company fundamentally has a choice between
taking over an existing building (and converting it to
meet its needs) or buying a greenfield site and putting a
building on it. Japanese companies in particular prefer
greenfield sites for their overseas direct investments.
(See **FDI**)

There are several advantages to greenfield sites:

- The building can be designed and built to suit the company's particular needs.

- The infrastructure is usually better and access to freeways, railheads, and so forth quicker and easier than from an older site nearer to the center of a town.

- There may be tax incentives to encourage investment and job creation.

The disadvantages:

- Public transportation is often lacking, and the company must organize its own.

- There are no shopping facilities nearby, so the company has to provide cafeterias and other conveniences.

### GREENMAIL

A once popular technique in takeovers whereby somebody bought a number of shares in a company and then threatened to make a public offer for all the company's stock . . . unless. The "unless" usually involved the company buying back the greenmailer's shares at a hugely inflated price.

So incensed did Americans become with this practice that legislators imposed a special greenmail tax on any gain made in this way.

### GROWTH SHARE MATRIX

A system for thinking about STRATEGY within a diversified corporation, the matrix plots each business's "growth" rate against its relative market "share." The grid made by these two axes is divided into four. Each of the four has a memorable name:

1. **Stars** are the high-growth, high-share businesses — these are ones to nurture with scarce resources.

2. **Dogs** are the low-growth, low-market-share businesses — these are ones to get rid of.

3. **Cash cows** are the low-growth, high-market-share businesses — these are to be bled for cash to feed the stars.

4. **Question marks** are the high-growth, low-market-share businesses. For these you need to bide your time and wait and see what they become. Cash cows generate cash by reaping the benefit of the EXPERIENCE CURVE.

The matrix suggests that the diversified company run its business as a portfolio. Developed by THE BOSTON CONSULTING GROUP, it is the most famous strategic tool to be invented in the last 30 years. But in practice it presents some difficulties.

• It is not always easy to find market share or even to define which market is relevant to the unit in question. So there is often doubt about a business's correct position on the horizontal axis.

• More fundamental, there are questions to be asked about the matrix's assumption that high market share gives better profitability than lower market share. Japanese companies have often gone for market share at the expense of profit.

As a result of these difficulties some companies have attempted to refine the basic matrix — companies such as GENERAL ELECTRIC and ROYAL DUTCH/SHELL, whose BUSINESS ATTRACTIVENESS/INDUSTRY STRENGTH matrix has nine squares rather than four, and slightly different axes.

### Harvesting

See DECLINING INDUSTRY

### Hay management consultants

The world's leading consultancy in human resources, founded by Edwin Hay, an American who was a pioneer in the science of job evaluation. He opened his consultancy in Philadelphia in 1947.

In 1984, with many of its founders aging, the consultancy was bought by the eagerly diversifying advertising agency Saatchi & Saatchi. Six years later, with Saatchi in serious financial difficulties, the consultancy was sold to its managers in a **MANAGEMENT BUYOUT** for about $80 million in cash.

At the basis of Hay's work is a methodology (called the Guide Chart and Profile method) of job evaluation. It defines the range of jobs within a corporation and the range of factors to be considered when evaluating these jobs. Edwin Hay had discovered a remarkable degree of commonality to jobs and the relevant factors required, regardless of company.

### Herfindahl index

See CONCENTRATION

### Hewlett-Packard

The giant computer company founded by Bill Hewlett and David Packard in a rented garage in California in 1938. Hewlett-Packard became particularly famous for its relaxed management style, described as MBWA — management by walking about. The company set the pace for the laid-back, quirky, individualistic, and hugely successful firms of Silicon Valley.

The company never had a grand VISION or a remarkable technological breakthrough to exploit. It started off making electronic instruments. One of its first orders was for audio oscillators for Walt Disney to use in the making of *Fantasia*. HP did not get into the computer business until the mid-1960s. The firm now has 90,000 employees around the world and annual sales of almost $15 billion.

Bill Hewlett has said that he cannot tell where the company will be in five years' time. HP once had a three-year plan, which it stuck to, but has never had anything longer. The computer industry, he says, "is not like making railroad cars. You have to be flexible and roll with the punches."

---

*Show competitors what you are doing. They will learn soon enough anyway. Just don't tell them what you are thinking.*

Bill Hewlett, co-founder of Hewlett-Packard

---

### HOCKEY STICK

A chart measuring projected sales over time that appeared in many corporate plans in the 1960s and 1970s. The forecast showed sales falling for a time before rising steeply; it looked like a hockey stick. The problem was that the managers could always pinpoint the cause of falling sales. They tended to be overoptimistic about how/why sales would rise again.

### HONDA

Founded in 1928 by Soichiro Honda, a car mechanic like Henry Ford, the company has become the world's leading manufacturer of motorcycles. Its 1959 entry into the American market has become a legend. Backed by the slogan "You meet the nicest people on a Honda," the company overturned the stereotype of motorcycle owners as greasy leather-jacketed unemployables.

From motorbikes the company has expanded into a range of products, all based on their CORE COMPETENCE, the combustion engine: cars, lawnmowers, outboard motors, and even snowblowers. Its Ohio car plant (opened in 1982) now exports vehicles to Japan.

The company has a clearly defined mission statement:

- Quality in all jobs — learn, think, analyze, evaluate, and improve.
- Reliable products — on time, with EXCELLENCE and consistency.
- Better communication — listen, ask, and speak up.

Its much-vaunted team approach to decision making is being reworked to help it meet the challenge from niftier car manufacturers that have been able to produce more exciting models more quickly.

### HORIZONTAL EXPANSION

This is the STRATEGY of expanding a company by going into lines and products that are sold to similar markets and in similar ways as the firm's existing product range. For example, a manufacturer of disposable pens might move into greeting cards — something that could be sold through the same sort of retail outlet. (See ECONOMIES OF SCOPE)

If the disposable pen company became worried about its supply of ink, and decided to expand into the manufacture of industrial ink for its own pens (and other people's), that would be a case of vertical expansion. (See INTEGRATION)

## HORIZONTAL INTEGRATION

See INTEGRATION

## HUMAN RESOURCE MANAGEMENT (HRM)

The personnel function turned from a Cinderella into a beautiful princess when it changed its name to human resource management. Companies began to appreciate that the relationship between management and other employees must flow both ways. Personnel dealt with a one-way relationship, reacting when things went wrong, when more staff were needed, when less staff were needed, or when pay scales had to be revised. Human resource management is about making the relationships among all employees work as effectively as possible.

Michael Porter says that human resource management is "the recruiting, training and development of personnel. Every activity [in industry] involves human resources, so human resource management spans the whole VALUE CHAIN." For Porter it is one of only three activities that do span the whole value chain: the others are technological development and procurement. Greater EMPLOYEE INVOLVEMENT and the challenge of MANAGING DIVERSITY have increased the strategic importance of the HRM function.

*The future prosperity of Sony rests in the hands of the last person we recruited.*

Akio Morita, Sony chairman

## IBM

The world's greatest computer company, with a market LEADERSHIP that was unmatched in any other significant industry. IBM grew up as a clean-cut American — short hair, blue suits, and ties were *de rigueur* for its managers. Now it is in the process of growing into a global firm without nationality, but it still stands by three basic beliefs:

1. Respect for the individual — it lays emphasis on EMPOWERMENT and says it is "putting a premium on autonomy." Until recently, this was backed up by a policy of lifetime employment.

2. EXCELLENCE. Time and again it has shown that it is not always the pioneers who win the race. It was not the first into the market for PCs, for example. But when it entered the market, it swept the board.

3. Superior customer service.

IBM is well known for its strong, monolithic CULTURE, supported by a superior management training program and a policy of promoting from within. However, some argue that its very strong corporate culture led the company to become insular and unresponsive to a changing market. In a dramatic break with tradition, IBM's new CEO, Louis V. Gerstner, has no prior industry experience.

As so often happens with industry giants, IBM developed an enormous bureaucracy. Believing that its market was protected by a huge installed base, the company turned insular, the pace of innovation slowed, and IBM underestimated important changes in its market. Fearing that personal computers would CANNIBALIZE mainframe profits, IBM was slow to develop this technology, leaving room for nimble startups like APPLE.

IBM also underestimated the strategic advantage of VERTICAL INTEGRATION in personal computers, which created such powerful companies as Intel, which supplies chips, and MICROSOFT, which provides operating systems software. These companies are bringing about a restructuring of the computer industry, which in turn has eroded IBM's dominant position.

---

*Image means personality. Products, like people, have personalities, and they can make or break them in the marketplace. The personality of a product is an amalgam of many things — its name, its packaging, its price, the style of its advertising, and above all the nature of the product itself.*

David Ogilvy, *Ogilvy on Advertising*

---

### INDUSTRIAL ESPIONAGE

It is said that Communist Eastern Europe used to gain far more from its commercial spying in the West than it ever did from its military espionage. This is partly because commercial secrets are much more difficult to protect than military secrets are. In the first place, patent and copyright laws are difficult to enforce across borders. Some industries (e.g., American software manufacturers and European fashion houses) waste no opportunity to pursue the theft of their intellectual property abroad. But it is a long, hard, expensive process. IBM is said to spend over $50 million a year on security measures aimed at preventing espionage.

In many cases it is extremely difficult to prove that a crime has taken place. One person charged with industrial espionage was found guilty only of stealing sheets of photocopy paper. The fact that they were covered with highly sensitive commercial information was not taken into account because there was no appropriate law against it. One of the big ironies here is how much intelligence can be acquired perfectly legally through the careful analysis of public documents.

### INDUSTRIAL LIFE CYCLE

Industries, like individual businesses (and, indeed, individuals), go through a cycle during their life — from young embryo to growing youth to mature industry to aging dodderer. For individual firms in an industry, each stage requires a different strategic approach. In growing industries, gaining MARKET SHARE is all important; in mature industries, controlling costs matters more.

The life-cycle concept has been somewhat discredited because it provides little prescriptive benefit to a firm. The duration of the stages in the cycle vary with different industries — the mature stage in the toy industry is generally very short; in the steel industry it is very long. And who is to say what stage in its life an industry is at? Is the computer industry mature — or still a young business with enormous growth potential? (See also PRODUCT LIFE CYCLE)

### INDUSTRY STRUCTURE

Factors such as the technical and economic features of its product, the number of competitors, the existence of substitute products, and the relationship between industry participants and their buyers and suppliers determine an industry's structure. Michael Porter identified five competitive forces resulting from an industry's structure that determine both industry profitability and strategies for COMPETITIVE ADVANTAGE for individual participants. These five forces are buyer power, supplier power, competitor rivalry, threat of potential entrants, and substitute products.

### INFORMATING

One of the most powerful new management ideas, now largely associated with the writings of Shoshana Zuboff, a Harvard Business School professor and author of *In the Age of the Smart Machine* (Basic Books, 1988). Informating is the process by which IT, information technology (the combination of computers and telecommunications) affects organizations and the way they function.

The idea starts from two principles:

1. Information technology is different from earlier technological developments in its effects on industry in at least one important respect: earlier technological breakthroughs enabled companies to automate various processes — and the hallmark of automation was a diminution in the quantity and quality of human labor. IT does not automate companies; rather it informates them, providing workers with access to information that empowers them to think and make decisions that they were not able to do before. Computerized stock control systems, for example, enable the person in the stockroom to decide what needs ordering and when. In the past

the decision would have been made by a senior manager in the head office, or information would have been passed by middle managers to the stockroom so that the decision could be made there.

2. The informated company has to operate in a way completely different from that of traditional companies. IT enables anybody in the corporation to have access to any information anywhere. That removes the need for those middle managers who do nothing but shuffle information from one place to another. Then it enables the company to reorganize itself so that decision making is decentralized away from senior managers at headquarters down to the employees on the front line. Ultimately, IT should enable all decision making to be done by ad hoc committees consisting of the people most appropriate for the job.

### INFORMATION TECHNOLOGY MANAGEMENT

The sharp decline in the cost of information systems (IS) technology (i.e., a combination of communications and computer technology), the development of user-friendly formats for nontechnical users, and the rapid spread of highly portable computer and communications devices have moved information technology from a support role to a potential source of significant competitive advantage.

F. Warren McFarlan, writing in the *Harvard Business Review* (May–June 1984) says IS technology is a strategic weapon if it can

- build BARRIERS TO ENTRY;
- lock in customers by creating switching costs;

- change the basis of **COMPETITION** by adding value, creating an opportunity for **DIFFERENTIATION**, or reducing cost;
- change the balance of power in supplier relationships; and
- generate new products.

---

*Innovation means taking a quantum leap beyond what is known and expected, to really produce a superior product.*

John Pepper, president, Procter & Gamble

---

## INNOVATION

---

*One should recognize and manage innovation as it really is — a tumultuous, somewhat random, interactive learning process, linking a worldwide network of knowledge sources to the subtle unpredictability of customers' end users.*

James Brian Quinn, "Large-Scale Innovation: Managing Chaos," *Tuck Today*, June 1985

---

To stay competitive in today's fast-paced competitive environment, innovation is a must. Product innovation opens new markets, creates opportunities for **DIFFERENTIATION**, and increases **MARKET SHARE**. Process innovation improves cost competitiveness. Innovation does not just happen, it needs to be encouraged at all levels of the organization. Corporations such as 3M and Raychem that make innovation a priority generate a substantial portion of corporate revenue through internally developed, often proprietary products.

Andrew J. Parsons of MCKINSEY suggests five steps for building innovative capabilities.

1. Diagnose the company's situation to assess whether, why, and where there is an innovation problem.

2. Determine how innovation fits into overall competitive strategy — for example, "big bang leader" or just a "fast follower."

3. Build special skills. Successful companies build the scientific, manufacturing, and marketing skills they need to innovate.

4. Use a cross-functional project such as teams to minimize resistance to change.

5. Manage the process.

### IN PLAY

A company is said to be "in play" when the stock market suspects that somebody is building up a stake in it with a view to making a bid. There are several things to be done by managers who suspect that their company is in play. These can be described as either offensive or defensive.

Offensive moves can include publicizing exciting new research findings or new investment plans; or can involve bringing forward the date of the announcement of good company results. All these would be aimed at increasing the company's share price in order to deter the suspected predator.

Defensive moves can include things like rewriting managers' contracts so that they become much more expensive under conditions that are triggered only if and when the company is taken over. Or they could include selling off bits of the company that are known to be particularly attractive. (See **CROWN JEWELS**)

### INSIDE INFORMATION

Information about the activities of a public company that is not known to the general public, but which is sufficiently significant to move the share price of the company were it to become known.

Typically, such information might be about an intended **TAKEOVER** of one company by another. In such takeovers the price being offered for the target company has to be higher than its stock market price because the bidder will not persuade shareholders to sell their shares unless it is. Thus anybody buying shares on the basis of inside information knows that he or she can sell them to the bidder soon after at a guaranteed profit. Since such takeovers require an extensive array of advisers — lawyers, bankers, and accountants — there is plenty of scope for information to leak out.

Anybody who acts on inside information for his or her own benefit with the knowledge that it is inside information is committing an offense in an increasing number of countries, including the United States and Britain. There is an argument that says using inside information should not be a crime because there is no victim. But that is not strictly true: the (unidentifiable) shareholder whose shares were bought by the insider dealer is the victim. (See also DISCLOSURE)

---

*Companies today are not like they were in Victorian times — properties with tangible assets worked by hands whose time owners bought. Business today depends largely on intellectual property, which resides inalienably in the hearts and heads of individuals.*

Charles Handy

---

## INTEGRATION

See VERTICAL INTEGRATION

## Johnson & Johnson (J&J)

With 166 separate operating companies, this pharmaceutical, consumer, and professional products company is built on a philosophy of **DECENTRALIZATION.** Johnson & Johnson believes that smaller self-governing units are more manageable, quicker to react to their markets, and more accountable. Although some units have been consolidated, and top management has tried to address some inefficiencies by centralizing such functions as payroll processing and computer services, J&J strives to retain a sense of ownership, an aggressive approach to marketing, and the freedom to be creative and innovative. Products introduced over the past five years account for 25% of sales.

Johnson & Johnson's most recent competitive success has been its market leadership in disposable contact lenses with Acuvue. In 1983, a J&J staffer in Europe learned of a new Danish technology for producing disposable lenses inexpensively. J&J moved quickly to develop packaging and a manufacturing process, building a high-volume mass-production lens plant in Florida. It marketed the lenses nationwide through an expensive advertising campaign at a time when competitors did not even have the production capacity to make competing brands available nationwide. The new product has succeeded because the decentralized unit could make important production and marketing decisions quickly, while enjoying access to a substantial corporate war chest unavailable to small startup companies.

## JOINT VENTURE

A form of alliance between two or more firms for the purpose of entering a new market or a new business. The joint venture is a well-established method for firms to spread the risk involved in such strategies. It often takes place between a firm with cash and another with expertise or contacts (or both). In some senses FRANCHISING is a form of joint venture.

Historically, joint ventures have been between non-competing firms — for example, between a MULTINATIONAL manufacturer and a local distributor in a country where the manufacturer is first setting up a new production plant, or in a country where the government insists that foreign investors have a local partner.

More recently, joint ventures have focused on the technological development of new products and have frequently been formed between firms that theoretically should be competing with one another. The electronics industry is a prime example, with Japanese and American firms and Japanese and European firms forming a spider's web of joint ventures for the development of new generations of semiconductors and new electronic consumer durables such as high-definition television (HDTV).

This peculiar phenomenon is explained mostly by the high cost of development involved in these products. No firm dare undertake such development without ensuring a respectable market presence at the end of it. Joint ventures may be particularly suitable for certain stages of the industrial cycle — for very young products and for very old ones, perhaps. If so, then all joint ventures need to be under constant surveillance in order to spot the time when their useful life is over.

*This joint venture gives both companies the ability to advance technologically without the cost burdens of acting independently.*

Toshiba on its joint venture with IBM

---

To work effectively, joint ventures need to have clear objectives, mutually understood by both partners. Managers assigned to the joint venture need to have incentives to make the venture succeed so that they are not torn by conflicting loyalties to the parent organization. Each partner needs to understand clearly what it wants from the venture. Finally, if the objectives are somewhat short-lived, such as learning or market entry, there should be a plan to end the relationship when these objectives have been met.

### JUST-IN-TIME (JIT)

In an effort to eliminate inventory carrying costs, TOY-OTA devised a production management system that would eliminate inventory by scheduling purchased materials to arrive as needed, even if this meant 10 times a day. Modern information technology makes this possible. A frequent criticism of JIT purchasing is that it only shifts the burden onto suppliers.

## Key Area Evaluation

A framework for evaluating businesses that has evolved from the work of Peter Drucker. He maintained that companies need to have objectives in eight key areas:

- Market standing
- **PRODUCTIVITY**
- Profitability
- Physical and financial resources
- **INNOVATION**
- Manager performance and development
- Employee performance and attitudes
- Public and social responsibility

The company needs to measure continually the extent to which it is (or is not) reaching the objectives that it has set itself in these eight areas.

## Kinked Demand Curve

The economic phenomenon whereby (for many markets) a small increase in the price of a company's product can result in a large drop in sales, while a small decrease in price can result in virtually no increase in sales. This gives a "kink" in the curve plotting demand against price at that price where the phenomenon occurs (known as a "sticky" price).

Kinked demand curves are common in industries that are largely national and that tend to be oligopolies — such as banking, gas retailing, or cinemas in their heyday. At almost any given gasoline price, a retailer will not be able to raise its prices out of line with the rest of the pack without risking empty pumps. If it unilaterally cuts its prices, however, it will find that the pack has been forced to follow its example so quickly that it has no time to reap any benefit from the initiative.

This situation puts firms under pressure to ensure that they are not left high and dry when an increase in costs forces them to make a price increase that none of their competitors has to follow. This raises the temptation for firms in such an OLIGOPOLY to collude. (See CARTEL)

### KLYNVELD PEAT MARWICK GOERDELER (KPMG)

The largest accounting firm in the world, and the only one of the Big Six not pot-bound in its Anglo-Saxon roots. KPMG is the result of a 1987 merger between KMG, an international federation of firms particularly strong in Holland and Germany, and Peat Marwick Mitchell, a firm established when Mr. Peat from London met Mr. Marwick from New York on a west-bound transatlantic liner in 1911.

KPMG has been trimming fat in recent years. It cut hundreds of partners from its payroll and (after a minor coup) appointed a new, young chairman for its all-important American operation. The chairman's name is Madonna — Jon Madonna.

## LBO

The widely used and much less widely understood acronym for "leveraged buyout" — a phenomenon in Britain and America in the 1980s whereby a company was bought by a group that incurred a large amount of debt to make the purchase. The company thus became highly leveraged (in other words, it had a large amount of debt compared to its equity). When the group doing the buying was made up of the company's managers, the LBO was also a **MANAGEMENT BUYOUT (MBO)**.

Banks were willing to finance LBOs because they had a new-found enthusiasm for lending to corporations, many of which they had decided at the time were under-borrowed compared with their capacity to service debt. But the capacity of many LBOs to service the debt they incurred was too often premised on an assumption that the future (the early 1990s) would be a replay of the past (the early 1980s). Two of the biggest LBOs put together by **SALOMON BROTHERS** in the late 1980s (Revco and Southland) have already ended up in Chapter 11 bankruptcy.

*As for the best leaders, people do not notice their existence. The next best, the people honor and praise. The next, the people fear; and the next, the people hate. When the best leader's work is done, the people say, "We did it ourselves."*

Lao Tzu, Chinese philosopher

## LEADERSHIP

This is either a corporate STRATEGY in which a firm aims to be the leader in a particular market (through superior price or quality); or it is a human quality that differentiates a chief executive from the most junior accountant.

There is one essential difference between leaders and managers: for good managers, systems and structure are all important; good leaders are unconventional and work outside systems, relying on a lot of intuition and at least a little inspiration. They can range from the obviously flamboyant Lee Iacocca to the unassuming (but highly effective) Sir Peter Holmes (at ROYAL DUTCH/ SHELL) and the many self-effacing leaders of successful Japanese companies.

John Kotter, a Harvard Business School professor, talks about a "leadership network," emphasizing that leadership is not something that is uniquely confined to the chief executive. It should be spread around the organization. DECENTRALIZATION makes the task of developing leaders that much easier because it creates plenty of jobs within the organization that require qualities of leadership. Jan Carlzon, chairman of SAS, says that the Scandinavian airline has 2,000 leaders.

The best leaders, Kotter maintains, have had a broad mix of jobs and responsibilities early in their careers. Other researchers into leadership support this view, and add that great leaders are often "only" children, brought up in cosmopolitan (or colonial) backgrounds. (See also COST LEADER and FOLLOWER)

---

*Most firms are overmanaged and underled.*

John Kotter

## LEAN PRODUCTION

A general term referring to a range of production techniques used (particularly by Japanese firms) to reduce costs and rapidly become hypercompetitive. They include techniques such as JUST-IN-TIME (JIT) manufacturing, computerized stock control, and TOTAL QUALITY MANAGEMENT (TQM).

## LEARNING CURVE

Practice may not necessarily make it perfect, but it does make it cheaper! Individuals as well as teams become better at performing any specific task with repetition. As early production problems are solved, quality improves, output increases, and costs decline. Strategists have applied this concept to define "experience" as a source of competitive advantage. (See EXPERIENCE CURVE)

## LEVERAGE

The ratio of a company's debt to its equity. There is no absolute level of leverage that is healthy for any particular industry. When analysts look at industry norms they tend to create a mythology about right or wrong levels that can in some cases become a constraint on a company's growth.

The important thing about leverage is that it highlights two very different forms of company finance: debt and equity. For example, the cost of debt — interest payments — is a fixed cost; the cost of equity — dividends — is not, at least in theory. These differences have a material effect on a company's strategy. Debt facilities are more easily arranged, and hence suitable for quick moves needed to seize brief market opportunities; equity is more stable and less demanding of instant returns, so it is more suitable for the long-term R&D needed to develop new products or processes.

---

*PepsiCo has a leverage "target." Over time the company aims to keep the ratio of net debt to net debt plus the market value of its equity to between 20% and 25%.*

PepsiCo Annual Report

---

## LICENSING

An important strategic decision for many firms is whether to license to another firm a technology, process, trademark, or patent that it has developed. The decision will be determined by different considerations. In some cases it will be forced on a firm by import restrictions that leave it with only one option: to grant a license to a local manufacturer allowing it to produce the product or service. Such licenses are usually granted for specific periods of time and contain stipulations about production equipment and output. This is to ensure that the brand is not devalued by inferior production or by illegal export.

Licenses are also granted for sound strategic reasons. A company may want to disseminate its technology as fast as possible in the hope that it will become a world-wide industry standard and thus outflank its rivals (as MATSUSHITA outflanked SONY and PHILIPS with their inferior videotape technology). The danger is that by spreading its proprietary technology so widely the company will spawn a host of competitors that it would not otherwise have had to cope with.

## LIFE CYCLE

See INDUSTRIAL LIFE CYCLE and PRODUCT LIFE CYCLE

### LIMITED PARTNERSHIP

A form of partnership particularly popular in Germany. Some of the partners (called the general partners) have unlimited liability, while others (the limited partners) have a liability that is limited to the amount of capital that they have agreed to put up. Only the general partners can be involved in the day-to-day management of the business.

This is an example of the way in which the rift between the ownership and management of business has developed differently in continental Europe from Anglo-Saxon nations. Limited partnerships provide a useful halfway house between the unlimited Anglo-Saxon partnership and the limited company. They make a clear distinction between the responsibilities that come with a manager's stake in a business and those that come to the pure owner/capitalist.

### LOGISTICS

The process of moving people and things about and of getting the right things in the right place at the right time — in the right amounts. That includes distribution, stock control, warehousing, packaging, and materials scheduling.

For many years logistics took a management back seat, looked on as a secondary activity that had to be seen to after more glamorous things like finance, MARKETING, and production had been dealt with. But the development of computer technology and the influence of production processes largely developed by the Japanese (such as JIT) have made many companies see logistics in a different light. Like anything that has been ignored for too long, it has become a key area for companies to gain COMPETITIVE ADVANTAGE.

## LONG-RANGE PLANNING

Companies used to spend much effort devising complicated corporate plans that tried to look way into the future. Such detailed long-term planning is currently out of favor. This is not only because of a growing realization of the futility of such planning in a world where CHANGE is occurring ever more quickly. It has also been influenced by a change of attitude toward planning itself — a switch to the identification of wide general trends (see also CORPORATE PLANNING) and a belief that line management should assume responsibility for its own planning.

---

*We're gonna stay on until the end of the world. And when that day comes we'll cover it, play "Nearer My God to Thee," and sign off.*

Ted Turner, founder of CNN

---

## MALCOLM BALDRIGE AWARD

The U.S. national quality award, named for a former secretary of commerce. Established in 1987, awards are given in three categories: manufacturing, service, and small business. Companies submit applications, detailing their quality practices in each of seven areas: **LEADERSHIP**, information and analysis, strategic quality planning, human resource utilization, quality assurance, quality results, and customer satisfaction. A team of examiners visits each finalist.

Originally intended to generate corporate interest in **QUALITY** programs and inspire national competitiveness, the award has stirred controversy. Former Baldrige examiners have opened lucrative consulting practices, taking as clients Baldridge aspirants. Some Baldrige winners experienced subsequent financial problems. Finally, applicants have invested significant amounts of time and money in the preparation of their applications, leaving critics to wonder if form has replaced substance in the search for quality. Quality guru David Garvin of the Harvard Business School believes that the Baldrige award has created a common vocabulary and philosophy bridging companies and industries. Companies have become willing to learn from one another and to improve quality.

## MANAGEMENT BUY-IN

The case where a team of managers buys into a company from outside it; a less common phenomenon than the similar **MANAGEMENT BUYOUT (MBO)**. As with the MBO, the purchase is backed by large amounts of debt. In a management buy-in there is an added uncertainty from not knowing how the incoming management team will interact with the existing staff — although in a number of cases the new team has been known to the existing one (as former managers, or as managers from a rival company).

## MANAGEMENT BUYOUT (MBO)

A TAKEOVER of a company in which a team of the company's managers becomes its owners by purchasing a controlling interest in the shares; banks then lend the company large sums of money to refinance it, money that is secured on the assets of the company. There was a great spate of MBOs in the easy-money years of the 1980s, many of which ran into difficulties in the higher-interest years of the 1990s.

MBOs are often seen as being appropriate for bits of large groups that have been put on the market because they are underperforming. But this raises the very pertinent question as to why the same management team should perform better when it has a share in the ownership of the company than when it was merely an agent of the owners. Companies in the same industry need to watch out for the strategic implications of a highly leveraged rival suddenly appearing in their midst.

### MANAGEMENT CONSULTANT

Consultants may never live down the description of them in Robert Townsend's *Up the Organization* as people who borrow your watch in order to tell you what time it is, and then walk off with the watch. Despite this unflattering image, the consulting business has grown dramatically in the past two decades. Much of that growth has come as an offshoot of the accountancy business. Since the 1970s, major consulting firms have hired top-ranked students from prestigious MBA programs. The relationship between major consulting firms and prominent business schools is a close one, resulting in a constant flow of both ideas and people.

The consultants' dilemma lies in how far to go in order to advise clients. Many have discovered to their cost that clients call them in, receive a bulky report and sheaves of recommendations, and then do absolutely nothing. The result? A lot of angry shareholders who see the huge fees paid to the consultants, and no change in their corporation.

Many consultants, therefore, like to have more of a hands-on role in implementing their recommendations. The trick is knowing how far to take this. Some companies actually have been run by outside consultants rather than by their own management.

The consulting market has become so large that it is already well segmented. One analysis suggests that it is breaking down into five sectors:

- **INFORMATION TECHNOLOGY MANAGEMENT**
- Manufacturing management, product development, and technology
- Organizational effectiveness (including finance, **MARKETING**, and **HUMAN RESOURCE MANAGEMENT**)
- Corporate **STRATEGY**
- Public-sector consulting

In recent years strategy consultancy has been the slowest growing of these five sectors. Information technology has been the fastest growing, probably at a rate of more than 30% a year in the last years of the 1980s.

## MANAGEMENT INFORMATION SYSTEMS

The panoply of systems (paper-based or electronic) that bring information to managers inside a company. In the past these systems focused on garnering internal information — about business units' budgets, or sales forecasts, or whatever. But recently they have switched to enabling managers to gather more information that is external to the company — about general economic conditions and about the behavior of competitors and consumers.

This switch has been affected by the increasing sophistication and the decreasing cost of information technology (IT), the heady mix of computers and telecommunications. IT enables any information to reach all parts of an organization simultaneously.

The question for senior managers is this: How much should be spread how far? There are electronic Luddites who would prefer to ignore IT and carry on as if paper pushing were as essential a part of the human condition as digging coal thousands of feet underground.

## MANAGEMENT STYLE

The general attitude taken by management to the discharge of its duties. Styles can vary from authoritarian to participative, embracing the MBWA (management by walking about) style of companies such as HEWLETT-PACKARD.

Some research has suggested that the most successful managers are those who vary their style to suit different situations.

## MANAGERIAL GRID

A system for analyzing managers along two dimensions: according to their concern for people, and according to their concern for completing tasks. Each dimension has scores from one to nine, so there are 81 different positions on the grid. They range from the 1,9 manager who is concerned with people to the 9,1 manager who is concerned with tasks.

It is not helpful to try to be too precise about this measurement. The grid is useful in making managers think about the two dimensions and (roughly) where they might fit on them.

*If I had to sum up in one word the qualities that make a good manager, I'd say that it all comes down to decisiveness. You can use the fanciest computers in the world and you can gather all the charts and numbers, but in the end you have to bring all your information together, set up a timetable, and act.*

Lee Iacocca

## MANAGING DIRECTOR

See CHAIRMAN and CHIEF EXECUTIVE OFFICER

## MANAGING DIVERSITY

*Managing diversity does not mean controlling or containing diversity, it means*

*enabling every member of your workforce to
perform at his or her potential.*

R. Roosevelt Thomas, Jr. "From Affirmative Action to
Affirming Diversity," *Harvard Business Review*
(March–April 1990)

---

Two trends are fueling this effort. First, global corporations unite employees from different national cultures. Second, in the United States over half of the workforce consists of women, minorities, and immigrants. The objective is not to assimilate minorities and women into a dominant white male culture but to create a new dominant heterogeneous culture.

### MARGINAL COST

The cost of producing one extra item. This is not the same as the average cost of production. Marginal cost ignores the cost of plant and equipment needed to produce the goods. When business is slack and a plant has considerable surplus capacity, the marginal cost is the very lowest price that a manufacturer can charge for his goods without actually incurring a loss.

The concept of prices and costs "at the margin" is a common one in economics and subsequently in business. For example, the marginal productivity of capital is the annual return earned by adding one extra unit of capital to an investment. The marginal propensity to consume is that percentage of one extra unit of income that a consumer will choose to spend rather than to save.

## MARKETING

All those processes associated with promoting and selling a product or service. Traditionally seen as one of the more glamorous parts of doing business.

## MARKET PENETRATION

Market penetration is the percentage of all potential customers for a product or service who have bought the product or service. A slightly different marketing concept, **MARKET SHARE**, refers to the percentage of those actual purchasers of the product who bought ones produced by the company.

A company seeking to increase its market penetration needs to concentrate on informing more people about its product — perhaps by improving or broadening the distribution network, by increased advertising, or by widespread special promotions. When market penetration is low, a company can increase a product's sales without taking market share from a competitor.

## MARKET SATURATION

When a product is launched successfully into a new market it can expect to sell large quantities until the market reaches saturation. Consider, for a moment, compact disc players. Until all households have one, sales will be considerable. Then they will settle back at the modest level at which consumers replace their existing models. Plotting sales against time for CD players shows up as an angled *S* curve.

Companies with products that face market saturation have to make some important strategic decisions. Should they sell as many products as they can early on? — a plan that involves building up large production capacity, much of which will be surplus when the market has reached saturation point.

Other companies decide not to build up capacity rapidly in the early years of the product's life but try instead to establish theirs as a premium product (with a considerably higher profit margin but lower sales), hoping that consumers will trade up to their premium product when it is time to buy a replacement. Thus they can come to dominate the replacement market without having to increase and reduce their production facilities like an inflatable balloon.

### MARKET SEGMENT

See SEGMENTATION

### MARKET SHARE

The percentage of all sales in a market accounted for by a single producer. The hard part of the analysis is defining the market correctly.

There has been much (and contradictory) evidence on the relationship between market share and profitability. Some studies have shown that they are related — as market share increases so does profitability; other studies have shown quite the opposite. The truth may be that the relationship varies according to the type of industry in question; for example, where there are significant ECONOMIES OF SCALE to be made (as in the car or consumer goods industries), then the size of market share could be expected to be positively related to profitability. In industries such as software, however, where there are more likely to be diseconomies of scale from increasing market share, the opposite may well be the case.

## MATRIX MANAGEMENT

A method of managing multinationals that was developed largely by the Dutch electronics company PHILIPS after World War II. It involved giving responsibility for bits of the company's activities to both the national organization and the product division (based in Holland). Lines of responsibility thus flowed horizontally and vertically, creating a matrix.

Within Philips, every manager had dual accountability — no one was solely responsible to one individual. This had obvious disadvantages; for example, it encouraged the creation of large numbers of decision-making committees, and it often left managers ambiguous about their aims. In the 1960s and 1970s Philips found that its national organizations were dominating the product divisions, and the company took steps to correct that by giving new responsibilities to the head-office divisions. By the end of the 1980s, the tables had turned and the product divisions were made ultimately responsible for all the company's operations around the world — thus, in effect, abandoning matrix management.

Nevertheless, many companies continue to use some such structure — even though they may not describe it so formally as Philips. Matrix management has been found to be particularly appropriate for specific projects (such as new product development), where close teamwork is required, and where there is a time limit to the project.

*Leaders in highly layered organizations are like people who wear several sweaters*

> *outside on a freezing winter day. They*
> *remain warm and comfortable, but are*
> *blissfully ignorant of the realities of*
> *their environment.*
>
> John Welch, chairman of General Electric

## MATSUSHITA

The world's leading consumer electronics company, much of whose manufacturing is done by public companies (such as JVC) in which it owns a majority stake. Matsushita developed the winning VHS formula for videocassette recorders, and 30% of its sales come from video equipment.

In the second half of the 1980s Matsushita was forced to expand production overseas as the appreciation of the yen against the dollar cut the competitiveness of exports from Japan. In the 1990s it has followed the STRATEGY of its great rival, SONY, paying $6.6 billion for MCA, a company that provides software (film studios, cable television channels, and book publishing, for example) without which Matsushita's hardware is as much fun as a Toyota without gasoline.

## MATURE INDUSTRY

An industry that relies on repeat buyers rather than first-time buyers, and where rivals' market shares do not change much over time. A classic case is the car industry in North America, Europe, and Japan.

Some would turn a mature industry into a DECLINING INDUSTRY by assuming there was no more worthwhile profit to be gained from it. But the Japanese have shown again and again that there are many ways to develop profitability within mature industries. One is to concentrate less on product development and more on process development, aiming to become the lowest-cost producer in an industry where price levels may be determined almost as much by tradition as by real underlying cost. In other areas, such as photography, the Japanese have been highly successful in a mature industry by introducing small technological improvements (automatic focusing, for example). These have persuaded consumers to abandon still-working old cameras and buy new ones.

## MAVERICK

A new entrant that adopts a strategy radically different from that of existing competitors in a market. This different strategy may be in the manufacturing process — as with the Italian clothing firm Benetton, which was able to revolutionize the dyeing process so that its garments were cut before they were dyed; or it may be in the distribution or retailing process — as with clothing firms that have tried to sell their products through supermarkets.

It is very difficult for an existing competitor in a market to become a maverick, but maverick strategy is often what is needed for successful change. The best hope may be for the firm to appoint a maverick-type individual as its chief executive.

## McKINSEY

The management consultancy firm founded by James McKinsey (1889–1937), an American who was professor of cost accounting at the University of Chicago business school. McKinsey was with the firm for only a few years in the 1920s (until he was offered the job of MANAGING DIRECTOR of Montgomery Ward). But his so-called General Survey, a checklist for effective management consulting, is still compulsory reading for all new McKinsey recruits.

McKinsey is undoubtedly a leader among strategy consultants, one-time employer of Tom Peters, Robert Waterman, Kenichi Ohmae, and Richard Pascale. McKinsey was the first to bring the American style of management consulting to the rest of the world. It brushed all COMPETITION aside when it first arrived in Europe in the 1950s. It was different: it focused on STRATEGY, and its lines of communication were with the top echelons of its clients while other consultants were grubbing around in the middle ranks.

McKinsey had substantial influence on the restructuring of American industry in the 1980s, trailblazing the fashion for returning to CORE COMPETENCE and eschewing DIVERSIFICATION. It advised, among others, CITICORP (the world's biggest bank — at the time); Merrill Lynch (the world's biggest securities firm — at the time); and GENERAL MOTORS (the world's biggest car company — at the time).

---

*Meetings are indispensable when you don't want to do anything.*

John Kenneth Galbraith

---

## MERCK

The remarkable pharmaceutical company that, under its long-time chairman and CEO Roy Vagelos, has headed

*Fortune*'s list of the most admired companies in America for six consecutive years. The world's largest and most profitable drug company, Merck has been the spawning ground for effective treatments for cholesterol, high blood pressure, and heart failure, among others.

The company's forte is R&D. Since 1980, a staff of scientists, researchers, clinicians, physicians, statisticians, and administrators that now numbers 4,500 has launched sixteen innovative drugs, the two most successful of which bring in over $1 billion annually.

With 17 research facilities around the world, Merck is operating as a **GLOBAL FIRM** and is moving from phased introduction of new drugs to simultaneous introduction in separate national markets.

Merck is forging **STRATEGIC ALLIANCES** to provide it with additional research, product lines, and **MARKETING**. It is also reinforcing the multidisciplinary teams that work on each project as it moves through the development process. Merck has discovered the potential benefit of aggressive investment in IT, using it to streamline and coordinate the final and most complex phase of the drug approval process: clinical trials, when drugs are tested on humans. In clinical trials, several hundred patients worldwide are tested for up to four years to determine proper dosage and to verify safety and effectiveness. Detailed records must be kept and analyzed. An ingenious computer and communications system, Clin-\*Net, specially programmed to spot inconsistencies in data, enables the company to better understand the status of clinical trials much earlier in the process.

### MICROSOFT

The software firm started by a couple of college kids playing around with BASIC computer language. One of those kids, Harvard drop-out Bill Gates, went on to become America's youngest billionaire.

Microsoft's big break came from being chosen in 1981 to provide the operating software (called MS-DOS) for IBM's personal computer. This software now runs on over 80 million different machines.

The company went public in 1986 and the following year had a phenomenally high P/E ratio of over 60. It has never paid a dividend — despite recording profits of $279 million in 1990 on sales of $1.18 billion.

Microsoft's next breakthrough project was Windows, a program that gives IBM PCs graphical capability similar to that of the APPLE Macintosh. Since then the company has achieved impressive successes in applications programs. The combination of operating systems leadership and new-found leadership in the applications arena led Microsoft to dominate the software industry. Some now compare it to IBM, and industry rivals complain about Microsoft's aggressive competitive tactics.

Despite its impressive size, Microsoft retains its distinctly nonbusinesslike culture.


#### Mission statement

A brief description of what an organization sees as its underlying purpose and values. The aim of such a statement is to give all employees a VISION that can carry them beyond their humdrum day-to-day tasks.

Despite the necessary "inspirational" element, mission statements should also have their feet firmly on the ground.

- They must reflect a consensus of what existing managers and staff believe they should be. It is no good creating a lofty statement that bears no relation to the art of the possible.

- They should not be taken as phrases from the Bible, sacrosanct and unchangeable. They must be alive, and they must grow and change with the company.

---

*Our mission is to achieve or enhance clear leadership, worldwide, in the existing or new core consumer product categories in which we choose to compete.*
*We believe that commitment to this mission . . . will enable the company to provide a superior return to our shareholders.*
Gillette

*Our mission is to be the most successful consumer packaged goods company in the world.*
*And our strategy to achieve this is by developing new products to meet emerging consumer trends, expanding geographically, and manufacturing and marketing globally.*
Philip Morris

---

### MULTINATIONAL

Sometimes called multidomestic, a multinational is an international firm run as a collection or portfolio of indi-

vidual domestic entities (often wholly owned subsidiaries), each with self-contained **MARKETING** and often
separate manufacturing facilities. In these vertical,
country-focused units, national management can lead
to significant differences in product lines across countries in an attempt to optimize profits within particular
domestic markets. In contrast to the **GLOBAL FIRM**, the
multinational has the opportunity to tailor products to
a national market, but it may miss the opportunities
for global competitive advantage through **ECONOMIES OF
SCALE.**

## NEGOTIATION

Negotiation is a fine art needed for the successful completion of any deal or contract. Styles of negotiation are strongly influenced by culture, and anybody negotiating with foreigners needs to be wary of assuming that he or she understands the meaning of any signals emanating from the other camp.

## NESTLÉ

The Swiss food company that has grown from humble origins in the small town of Vevey to become one of the world's great global firms, owner (*inter alia*) of Nescafé, Carnation, Findus, and Chambourcy. Founded by Henri Nestlé in 1866, its distinctive logo of a bird in a nest is now recognized all over the world.

The company had made a number of significant acquisitions, including Source Perrier and Carnation (acquired in 1985). In an uncharacteristic move, this conservative Swiss company has formed a **JOINT VENTURE** with **COCA-COLA** to produce canned coffee and tea drinks and another with General Mills to manufacture cereals.

*Henri Nestlé's pioneering approach embraced closer co-operation with the scientific world, advice to suppliers, his intelligent use and defense of his trademark, his far-sighted attitude, and his early experience as an exporter.*

Nestlé official history

## NET PRESENT VALUE

A useful quantitative estimate of the value today of a future project. The central premise is that cash received next week or next year is worth less than cash received today. Therefore future cash payments are discounted by a rate equal to what the analyst believes is the firm's COST OF CAPITAL. This estimate is a critical part of the analysis. Net present value is the sum of all the future cash flowing from a project (discounted to take account of the time when the cash is received), less all the costs to be incurred by the project (again discounted to take account of the time when they will be incurred).

This quantitative measure should not be taken too literally — it is only a guide as to the relative merits of various projects, and only one of several tools to be used for, say, CAPITAL BUDGETING.

## NICHE STRATEGY

A company that plans to serve only a small segment of a larger market is said to be following a niche strategy. For example, garment manufacturers who sell to the "larger" man or woman; or retailers who sell only socks, or ties, or underwear. Once they have identified their niche, such companies can still pursue a strategy of being the leader in that niche.

There are a number of advantages to a niche strategy:

- There is less COMPETITION; many larger competitors may ignore the market altogether since it does not make economic sense for them to serve it properly.

- It gives the company a clearer focus, which can help employees identify more easily with it. (See FOCUSING)

- It enables the company to gain a specialist skill and knowledge appropriate to the niche. This is not only useful in fending off competition, but it might also enable the specialist to add a premium to its prices for its special skill.

- The main danger of such a strategy is that the chosen niche will disappear as consumers and their habits change. While some clothes retailing has been broken off into new niches (like socks), other old established niches have been embraced by new forms of retailing.

### NONVOTING SHARES

There is a fundamental divide between nations that believe all shareholders should be equal and those that believe some should be more equal than others. The egalitarians are found mostly in Anglo-Saxon economies where stock markets are strong and well established, for it is stock markets, above all others, that abhor the inequality of shareholders.

In continental Europe in particular, companies can have a number of "classes" of shareholders. Some may have limited voting rights (one vote for every five shares held, say) and some may have no voting rights at all (nonvoting shares). The proliferation of disenfranchised nonvoting shares enables small coteries to retain control of a company while spreading the capital risk among a much larger group.

## OBJECTIVES

These are the medium-term goals toward which a company strives. At their best, objectives help employees attain levels of performance that they did not believe they were capable of. Objectives also provide yardsticks by which a firm can measure its success in fulfilling a strategy.

The best objectives have five qualities. They must be

- precise,
- measurable,
- feasible (that is, achievable),
- consistent, and
- suitable to the type of company and industry for which they were designed.

---

*Many assume that half efforts can be effective. A small jump is easier than a large one. But no one wishing to cross a wide ditch would cross half of it first.*

Karl von Clausewitz

---

## OFF BALANCE SHEET

For several reasons, some industries lay great store by doing business that does not necessitate any change in their balance sheet. This applies particularly to banks and other financial institutions. Such institutions have to conform to strict ratios imposed by central banks.

These ratios put ceilings on the amount by which one part of their assets or liabilities can increase without a corresponding increase in another balance-sheet item — usually their capital. To get around these constraints, ambitious financial institutions have searched for types of business that do not impose this type of cost. For the most part, such business consists of various types of consultancy or brokerage.

### OLIGOPOLY

When fewer than half a dozen firms dominate an industry or market, they are said to constitute an oligopoly. The behavior of such firms differs from that of those in markets where hundreds of companies are competing for business. It differs first and foremost because of the high degree of interdependence between the firms — whatever one does materially affects all the others. Competitive rivalry will be high. This puts a premium on gamesmanship (see **GAME THEORY**), where no move can be made without fully considering all the possible next moves of the **COMPETITION**.

Typically, oligopolies occur in detergent manufacture, gas retailing, and air transport (on any one route). Such markets are characterized by a difficulty in competing on price. So nonprice forms of competition (special offers, new launches, and so forth) are commonplace. (See also **CONCENTRATION**)

### OPERATING LEVERAGE

A company's fixed costs expressed as a percentage of its total costs. When this is high, companies have to try to use their **CAPACITY** as fully as possible. Competitors with high operating leverage may have lower costs at full capacity than less highly leveled rivals. However, in an economic downturn fixed costs remain, and they will be encouraged to take on any business that will make a contribution to their fixed costs — that is, at a price above **MARGINAL COST**. Less highly leveled competitors, while theoretically better able to weather a downturn, will have to deal with price competition from rivals desperate to cover fixed costs.

### ORGANIC GROWTH

Organic growth, the internal growth of a corporation by expanding on its existing resources, is seen today as a form of growth preferable to such alternatives as takeovers or joint ventures. Organic growth involves much less disruption in a company and its culture, and it is less likely to disappear than is growth attained by **TAKEOVER.**

Firms that grow organically very rapidly (in terms of increases in sales) often find that growth is achieved at the expense of profitability. Any growth requires investment in people and plant, and this cuts profit. This is okay if growth is occurring in order to achieve even higher profits in the future. But all too often, growth in turnover seems to occur purely for its own sake.

## Pac-man defense

A **TAKEOVER** in which the target company bites back and makes an offer to take over the shares of the suitor. The name is derived from a popular video game. (See also **REVERSE TAKEOVER**)

---

*Those who cannot remember the past are doomed to repeat it.*

George Santayana

---

## Partnering

See **ALLIANCE**

## Payback period

The time it takes for an investment project to pay for itself. Thus if an initial capital investment of $1 million produces an income stream of $250,000 every other year, the payback period is eight years.

This measure is sometimes used to compare one investment project with another — the one with the shorter payback period being preferred. The advantage of this method is its extreme simplicity; anyone can understand it. After a period in the strategic wilderness it has made a comeback in popularity.

Its disadvantage is that it takes no account of the time factor — when the money is paid back. A repayment of $250,000 every other year is not equivalent to $950,000 after one year and $50,000 after nine years, yet these two repayment schedules have the same payback period.

Moreover, the payback period takes no account of cash to be received after the period. Suppose the repayment of $950,000 were to be followed by another $950,000 after 10 years. Clearly the payback period has limited use as a tool for comparing investments and should be used only with other measuring rods.

## PepsiCo

The cola manufacturer appropriately headquartered in the town of Purchase, New York, PepsiCo has proved, above all others, that it is possible to be second in a market and still win.

Pepsi has always sold less cola than the Coca-Cola company, and that has encouraged it to diversify further. PepsiCo owns Pizza Hut, Frito-Lay, Kentucky Fried Chicken, and Taco Bell. Its total sales are considerably greater than Coca-Cola's, and only 36% of them come from soft drinks, compared with 84% at Coca-Cola. PepsiCo has no less than eight brands that generate sales of more than $1 billion a year.

PepsiCo is a leader in its noncola businesses: with 15,000 units, its restaurant business has more eateries than McDonald's, while Frito-Lay controls half of the market for salty snacks in the United States and enjoys operating margins of 20%.

PepsiCo has achieved success through innovative, well-executed management techniques. Not satisfied to merely react to competitors' moves, it will revamp operations, MARKETING, or management simply to stay a step ahead of the competition.

CEO Wayne Calloway identifies three main ingredients in the PepsiCo formula: "Love change, learn to dance, and leave J. Edgar Hoover behind." Learning to dance means finding new ways to deal with customers; in practice, this means a relentless push into new distribution channels. The reference to the late FBI chief means that managers are given a great deal of flexibility: Calloway sets aggressive financial goals and offers high salaries to get the best out of his managers.

One of PepsiCo's subsidiaries, Frito-Lay, is revolutionizing food distribution with a sophisticated information system that enables it to tailor its product mix by store to maximize sales. Its 10,000 salespeople carry hand-held computers that provide instant sales data broken down by store, location, and region for each product. These analyses are relayed to the delivery people, who use them to advise retailers how to stock their shelves most profitably.

### PERRIER

The French company, recently purchased by Nestlé, that produces the world's best-known "natural" water from a source near Vergeze that was known to Hannibal and Caesar before Dr. Perrier began to exploit it commercially in 1888.

In February 1990, Perrier had the "opportunity" to become one of the great exponents of CRISIS MANAGE-MENT, in something now referred to by the company as "L'Incident Benzene." At a time when it was the market leader by far in the United States, authorities there detected small quantities of (carcinogenic) benzene in samples of Perrier water. The company immediately withdrew all its products from the market and withheld supplies for several months. It destroyed FFr1 billion worth of the stuff, and incurred other costs of FFr250 million.

But when the product was relaunched, Perrier leapt to new levels of popularity, so much so that the company soon became the object of a fierce takeover battle between Nestlé (the winner) and various European interests grouped around Fiat and the Agnelli family. The surprisingly diversified Perrier is now concentrating on building up its two main businesses — in mineral water and cheese (it owns the Roquefort brand).

## PERT

An acronym for Program Evaluation and Review Technique (also called **CRITICAL PATH ANALYSIS**), a system designed by the consultants **BOOZ, ALLEN & HAMILTON** for the U.S. Navy and Lockheed. It was a way of ensuring that all the many components that went into weapons manufacture came together at the right time. First used in 1958, it was a sort of prehistoric **JIT** (**JUST-IN-TIME**, the Japanese system of controlling the flow of components that became widely popular in the 1980s).

## THE PETER PRINCIPLE

A principle enunciated by Laurence J. Peter, a Canadian professor of education in his book of the same name, co-authored with Raymond Hull: "In a hierarchy every employee tends to rise to his level of incompetence." It has been embraced so widely as a piece of management folklore that it clearly holds the grain of a great truth about organizational structures. For as long as organizations reward good work with promotion to a more "senior" job (and rarely punish bad work with demotion), they are sure to be full of people doing jobs they are not equipped for. The only people doing jobs well will be those who are just about to be promoted into incompetence, or those who cannot be promoted any further.

One way to avoid this is to promote people as far as possible without changing their jobs. Put them on different pay scales, change their job titles and their offices, but let them do the same work.

### PHILIPS

The great Dutch electronics firm whose centenary in 1991 saw one of the worst patches in its 100-year history. It announced losses of $2.68 billion for 1990, demonstrating the extent to which it had lost the competitive battle against Japan's consumer-electronics giants like SONY and MATSUSHITA.

Philips's R&D has traditionally been second to none: the company produced the first CD and a video recording system technically superior to that of the Japanese. But it was invariably beaten in the MARKETING of its products.

In 1990, it set out on a worldwide revitalization program, which it called Operation Centurion. It restructured its management (see MATRIX MANAGEMENT), sold off a bunch of businesses — including its stake in Whirlpool, a white-goods manufacturer, and its ailing computer division — and chopped over 50,000 employees off its payroll.

---

*One does not plan and then try to make the circumstances fit those plans. One tries to make plans fit the circumstances.*

General George Patton

---

### POISON PILL

A range of devices designed to make a TAKEOVER unpalatable to the swallower (that is, the acquirer). For example, a company might borrow a large sum of money in order to distribute it immediately as dividends to its shareholders; or it might issue a preferred stock that gives shareholders the right to redeem it at a hefty premium after a takeover. (See also CROWN JEWELS, PAC-MAN DEFENSE, SCORCHED-EARTH DEFENSE, SHARK REPELLANT)

### POLITICAL RISK

The degree of risk in a contract due to political factors: the chance that an overseas loan will not be repaid because the relevant government suddenly slaps on severe exchange controls, for example, or that a foreign contract will not be finished because of the election of a new government with contrary ideas.

Most major exporting nations have set up government-funded agencies to protect their exporters against certain specific (and common) political risks. Some industries are more prone to such risk than others — mining, for example, is a popular target of expropriating/nationalizing governments.

### PORTFOLIO MANAGEMENT

The study of how best to manage a portfolio of businesses under one corporate umbrella. In its early years this was mostly a matter of rechanneling cash within the firm — as prescribed by the best-known portfolio management technique of all, BCG's GROWTH SHARE MATRIX, the CASH COW of a group would be used to finance cash-hungry developments elsewhere. Today portfolio management is more concerned with looking for ways to exploit a company's **CORE COMPETENCE** in new areas.

The old style of portfolio management saw the group as a sort of bank. But in countries where capital markets and the banking system work properly, it should be economically inefficient for a nonfinancial company to work in this way. Cash cows should redistribute their surplus cash to their investors for them to reinvest through efficient capital markets.

This does not always happen, for several reasons:

- Companies fear redistributing one-off surplus cash to investors because, if they cannot repeat the distribution, investors can be ruthlessly ungrateful.

- While capital markets may be generally efficient, there are specific periods of time when they are not. For example, in the 1980s, as the United States was deregulating its banking system, notorious inefficiencies arose. These led to the rapid growth of new financial instruments (commercial paper, for example — a short-term market for passing surplus cash from a firm that has it to one that hasn't).

### PRESIDENT

See **CHAIRMAN**

### PRICE LEADER

That firm that takes the initiative in raising (or cutting) prices in an industry. In reality, most companies have little freedom to set the price of their own products; they cannot do much more than follow the industry leader. In most industries this will not be continually the same firm. Two or three firms might take turns in being price leader. This practice is found most frequently in an **OLIGOPOLY**.

When one firm is essentially a monopoly supplier, it will always be the price leader. The marginalized competition will have no choice but to follow. In any other situation there are important strategic consequences to being a price leader. The leader has to be sure that the competition will follow, and within a suitable length of time. If not, consumers may switch to competitors' products because of the price difference and then remain faithful to the competition once prices are again equalized.

If competitors hold off from following the leader for too long, then the leader may be forced to cut prices back to those of the pack. Such behavior is typical of commodity-type products (e.g., gasoline) that are highly price sensitive. It can also occur with financial products although there are many financial products (such as bank accounts) that are notoriously insensitive to price changes. (See also **COST LEADER**)

---

*People of the same trade seldom meet together, even for merriment and diversion, but the conversation ends in a conspiracy against the public, or in some contrivance to raise prices.*

Adam Smith

---

## PROBABILITY

A branch of mathematics of great interest to gamblers and croupiers. It consists of models of phenomena that occur unpredictably but are one among a number of known possible outcomes. There are many such phenomena in the business world; for example, the defective goods produced by a machine, or the sales of a company's products in a shop. Mathematical models can help predict the probability of these phenomena occurring, based either on past experience or on subjective judgment.

## PROCTER & GAMBLE (P&G)

The manufacturer of such familiar consumer brands as Tide, Crest, and Pampers, P&G has become a byword for MARKETING. Based at One Procter & Gamble Plaza, Cincinnati, Ohio, it is, like so many companies, closely associated with the fortunes of one town. (Coca-Cola's address is One Coca-Cola Plaza, Atlanta, Georgia.)

Founded in 1837 through a merger of the candle-making business of Mr. Procter and the soap-making business of Mr. Gamble, P&G was one of the first big advertisers. Today it is consistently one of the biggest corporate spenders on advertising in every major nation. It is also the world leader in detergents and disposable diapers. It has a great rivalry with UNILEVER in the long-running soap-suds wars.

## PRODUCTIVITY

Literally, the output produced by a unit of one of the three factors of production within a given period of time: thus there is the productivity of labor (the output per employee), the productivity of land, and the productivity of capital.

For the most part, increasing productivity is a gradual process of improvement. But occasionally there are inventions that allow a quantum leap in productivity: the computer, for example, improves dramatically the productivity of the office worker; the freeway improves the productivity of the truck driver; a new financial market (like the commercial paper market) improves the productivity of capital; and a new fertilizer or strain of seed can improve the productivity of land dramatically.

## PRODUCT LIFE CYCLE

Most products are born, live for a number of years, and then die. Like plants, products have an embryonic stage followed by growth, maturity, and eventual decline. The STRATEGY for each phase differs, and for some the life cycle is shorter than it is for others. For example, fashion goods such as the latest Paris *haute couture* experience a very short life cycle; but the life cycle of the cornflake is already more than a century long.

Other cycles can be identified within the life of a product. For example, a common cycle for many electronic goods in recent years has been that of domestic production, export, overseas investment and production, and then import back to the original producing country.

The strategy for launching a new product must be determined to some extent by its expected life cycle. If it is clearly a fashion product, then there is little time to develop its market through testing and controlled pricing. Short-term profit maximization is the name of the game. Products that could be on shelves for a century demand a more measured approach. (See also INDUSTRIAL LIFE CYCLE)

## PROFIT CENTER

A discrete unit within an organization that is responsible for its own profit; in other words, a unit that can produce its own self-contained P&L account. In theory, such centers encourage managers to be entrepreneurial and more responsible. In practice, no unit is an island, and there are always certain decisions affecting the bottom line of a profit center that are outside its control (decisions on intergroup pricing, for example). This can create internal resentment sufficient to outweigh the advantage of entrepreneurial responsibility.

## PROFIT IMPACT OF MARKET STRATEGY (PIMS)

This is a sophisticated service that was originally based on research by GENERAL ELECTRIC. Companies pay a fee to PIMS to become a member and then provide commercially sensitive information for each individual business on a confidential basis to the PIMS database.

This is fed into a computer, along with similar information from a large number of other businesses, and the computer uses the data to find relationships between strategy choices and commercial success or failure. Among the factors looked at are things like the relation between MARKET SHARE, quality R&D expenditure, degree of DIVERSIFICATION, advertising expenditure, and return on investment.

Members of PIMS then have access to the (anonymous) aggregated data generated by the computer. This cannot tell a company what STRATEGY it should pursue; but it can be a useful pointer as to which factors might be more relevant to an individual company's situation.

## PROTECTIONISM

Industrialists who claim that they are not protectionists at heart are probably lying. There is no easier business life than being a manufacturer behind high tariff walls, supplying an unsophisticated market with basic goods.

All governments who professedly pursue free-trade policies find themselves at times in conflict with those who are supposed to be the biggest gainers from those policies, their own nation's businesspeople. This applies equally to Italians and to Thais, to Peruvians and to Swedes.

### PROXY FIGHT

A fight during a TAKEOVER for the "proxy votes" of shareholders (that is, written authority giving others the power to vote on their behalf). If the acquiring company can obtain enough proxy votes, it can use them to appoint its own top management team and gain control of the company before actually buying it.

### PUBLIC RELATIONS

The business of communicating messages from a corporation to various audiences, while maintaining good relations with them. The audiences range from the business's suppliers to its employees, from its investors to its distributors, and from pressure groups to customers (although most communication with a business's customers is called advertising).

The means at the public relations manager's disposal include press releases, house magazines, annual reports, public speeches, and company videos.

### PUMP PRIMING

That extra bit of effort and energy required to get a pump flowing, after which it carries on smoothly and effortlessly, has an obvious analogy in business. Whether it be for an entirely new business or a new development in a large old business, pump priming is essential. Unfortunately, the need for that initial extra effort (that is, cost) comes at the most risky time in the **PRODUCT LIFE CYCLE**.

## PURCHASING

The buying of resources needed for the running of a business. In many companies attention is focused on the purchasing of major raw materials such as steel or cloth or semiconductors. But these may not be the most expensive items that are purchased. Chrysler, for example, once discovered that it was spending more on health insurance for its employees than it was on any other single item. Yet the purchasing of this insurance had been delegated to a very junior manager.

The aim of purchasing is often said to lie in achieving the five rights: the right quality, the right quantity, at the right time, in the right place, at the right price. To those can be added a sixth: on the right terms.

The strategy question is how best to achieve these. Is it better to play suppliers off against one another, relying on **COMPETITION** to get the best price? Or is it better to encourage suppliers to cooperate and aim to get good prices because they know they have a long-term stable relationship with you? (This is the style favored by many Japanese companies, which traditionally have very close relationships with their suppliers.) Or is it better to rely on one supplier only, and make **ECONOMIES OF SCALE** by bulk buying? Does it pay to get involved with the suppliers' business to make savings? The answers to these questions are different for every business.

## QUALITY

David Garvin in *Managing Quality* (Free Press, 1988) advocates a **STRATEGY** that encompasses eight different dimensions of quality: performance, features (add-ons), reliability, conformance (to specifications), durability, serviceability, aesthetics, and perceived quality. Some of these are mutually reinforcing, some are not. A company cannot realistically compete on all eight. It is therefore important to choose dimensions that are important to the consumer and focus the effort where it creates a **COMPETITIVE ADVANTAGE**.

## QUALITY MANAGEMENT

In the 1980s the West became fascinated with Japanese methods of quality control, with quality circles (small groups of workers who gather together to discuss quality problems and search for solutions), and with total quality management (ways of permeating a whole organization with the goal of quality).

As these ideas filtered across the Pacific Ocean (via companies like Lockheed), Americans assumed that they had discovered the secret of Japan's industrial success. But these ideas had gone full circle. They had been carried from the United States to Japan in the early postwar years by men such as W. Edwards Deming and T. M. Juran.

They had based their thinking on a quantitative statistical approach to quality control, in particular on SQC (statistical quality control), a method developed in the famous Bell Laboratories in the 1930s. SQC goes back to ergonomics and early mechanistic concepts of management. It tries to analyze rigorously and objectively the levels of **PRODUCTIVITY** and quality that can be expected from a given production process. These become target levels, and the company very carefully monitors actual production in order to see how far it falls short of the targets. One of the main tasks of quality circles is to find out why quality standards are falling below the norm.

Quality circles have not enjoyed the same success in America and Europe as they have in Japan. Commenting on this in 1990, Peter Drucker, an American management guru, noted that

> *most U.S. quality circles of the past 20 years have failed despite great enthusiasm, especially on the part of the workers. The reason? They were established without SQC, that is, rigorous and reliable feedback.*

## RATE OF RETURN (ROR)

There are a number of useful measures of a company's rate of return — that is, the rate at which it is making money. They include the following:

- **Return on sales,** a simple measure of the percentage of each item sold that is retained as profit
- **Return on net assets,** a measure of the profitability of the assets employed by the company
- **Return on equity,** the basic return to shareholders

## REENGINEERING

Reengineering is the "fundamental rethinking and radical redesign of BUSINESS PROCESSES to achieve dramatic improvements in critical contemporary measures of performance such as cost, QUALITY, service, and speed," according to Dr. Michael Hammer and James Champy, chairman of CSC/INDEX, Inc. In their book *Reengineering the Corporation* (HarperBusiness, 1993), they state that reengineering requires

- reassessing the tacit rules and assumptions that govern the way a business is run — often they are obsolete; and
- disregarding all existing structures and procedures to find opportunities for major change which leads to dramatic improvement.

Automation and information technology are integral parts of reengineering, but the key to success lies in rethinking the entire process before automating individual tasks within it. Ford Motor Company reengineered its accounts payable department in the early 1980s and as a result reduced the staff involved in vendor payment from 500 to 125. An on-line database used for purchasing, receiving, and accounts payable has eliminated invoices entirely.

## REGRESSION ANALYSIS

A statistical technique for finding the "best fit" of a series of plots made on a chart. It has many applications in business. For example, consider a number of readings of sales figures for a certain product at a number of different prices. These readings may seem to be randomly spread about a tendency for higher prices to mean lower sales. Regression analysis finds the line that is the closest fit to all the readings. Extrapolating this line gives the best guess for what the product's sales will be at a particular price level.

Multiple regression analysis plots the relationship between the dependent variable and a number of independent variables. When a relationship is established, the dependent variable can be forecast using available data on the independent variables. Regression analysis is used frequently for demand forecasting. The demand for residential roofing shingles is related to new home starts and replacement demand.

Regression analysis needs to be applied judiciously. A mathematical correlation can be established between almost any two variables, but this does not necessarily establish a causal connection. Further, statistical analyses of historical data cannot deal with important competitive events such as the appearance of new rivals, technological breakthroughs, or abrupt changes in consumer taste.

## REGULATION

The intervention in the running of private businesses by government or its agencies. The ultimate form of regulation is nationalization. Short of that, governments regulate businesses and business activity in an almost infinite number of ways — from standardizing labels to approving pricing policy.

Certain sectors of the economy are more vulnerable to regulation than others. For example:

- **Banking.** In order to preserve the health of the financial system, every country has an official bank regulator (often the central bank).
- **Food manufacturing.** To preserve the health of consumers. The Food and Drug Administration (FDA) recently compelled PROCTER & GAMBLE to remove the word "fresh" from its Citrus Hill orange juice, and its "no cholesterol" claims from many of its products.
- **De facto monopolies.** To preserve the health of the consumer's pocket. In Britain the telecommunications industry (monopolized by British Telecom) is regulated by an official government body called Oftel, which has not stopped British Telecom from making annual profits of over £3 billion.

## REMUNERATION COMMITTEE

A subcommittee of a company's BOARD charged with responsibility for deciding on the pay of the board members (executive and nonexecutive). Most large companies have such committees. They commonly consist of the CHIEF EXECUTIVE OFFICER, a number of nonexecutive directors, and the head of human resources. Committees provide recommendations that are passed on to the **CHAIRMAN** of the full board.

Such committees address the problem of who is to decide on the salaries of those who decide on the salaries of everybody else. They are proliferating alongside rising criticism in the United States and Europe about the level of top managers' pay in relation to that of other employees, and in relation to relative pay scales in Japan. Japanese managers find the ratio of top pay to average pay in America and Europe shockingly high. They believe it is a serious disincentive to **PRODUCTIVITY**.

## REPLACEMENT DEMAND

Sales of new consumer durables (like video recorders) reach a sort of saturation point. This occurs when virtually all households that are likely to buy one of these products have already done so. Henceforth sales in such markets have to depend on the level of replacement demand.

Fast-moving consumer goods (like food or toothpaste) do not have this problem, for they never have any demand other than replacement demand.

Manufacturers of consumer durables have several ways of stimulating replacement demand — once they have penetrated new markets abroad with their products.

• They can introduce new technological developments — faster processing in the personal computer or lighter batteries in the portable computer, for example, that persuade consumers to switch to the new model and to ditch the old one. This is a double-edged option because the more the product is improved, the more marginal any future improvement begins to look.

- They can introduce new design features so that old models look "old fashioned." Alpine skis change color and design almost every year, making it obvious who is wearing last year's skis.

## REPOSITIONING

This is the process of altering a product's position vis-à-vis its market. Repositioning occurs continuously but is almost unobserved. As new entrants come into a market, the existing products or services are compelled to change their position slightly.

Repositioning can also occur, however, as a discrete strategic move. A company that anticipates how a market is changing may change its product accordingly. For example, a property developer on the Mediterranean who built small housing units as holiday homes for young local families may find that his market has shifted to elderly empty nesters from northern Europe. His whole marketing strategy has to change from selling access to sea, sun, and sand to selling access to golf courses and home help.

## RESIDENCE

An increasingly outdated concept that establishes which tax authority a company is primarily governed by. Since residence can mean different things in different places, a company can find itself resident in two places at once, with nasty fiscal consequences.

Corporations are resident in the United States if they are incorporated under the laws of any state. The European Community has tried to create a structure for a truly European corporation that will not be deemed as resident in any individual member state. But it has proved remarkably difficult to lift the idea of the corporation above the constraints of the nation-state.

## RESOURCE ALLOCATION

The process of deciding how to spread corporate financial resources among various businesses. This was especially complicated in the heyday of the diversified corporation when models such as the GROWTH SHARE MATRIX and the BUSINESS ATTRACTIVENESS/INDUSTRY STRENGTH MATRIX were developed. In today's more integrated corporation these decisions still need to be made. The outright competition between businesses or functions, however, has been replaced by a more cooperative approach.

## REVERSE TAKEOVER

When a company that is being bid for launches a successful takeover bid for the company that is bidding for it. Since most takeovers are of smaller companies by larger ones, reverse takeovers usually involve smaller companies taking over bigger ones.

If the bid is an all-paper offer (i.e., a question of swapping each other's shares), then the ownership may not be different whichever way the takeover goes. The main difference, then, in a reverse takeover is that the management of the smaller company calls the shots.

## RISK

The potential for loss if a project fails. One of the fundamental laws of business is that risk and return are related — that is, the riskier the investment, the bigger the return or reward if it succeeds. This is necessary because most people are risk averse: they prefer certainty to uncertainty. To persuade them to invest in an uncertain project, the promised return has to be large enough to overcome their reluctance. This is true for businesses as well as individuals.

## ROYAL DUTCH/SHELL

A collection of many hundreds of units in over 100 countries, each engaged in the business of discovering, mining, refining, and marketing oil and oil-related products. Each unit is 40% owned by the U.K. company Shell Transport and Trading, and 60% owned by the Dutch company Royal Dutch Petroleum, in one of those complicated Anglo-Dutch corporate combinations that work so well (see also UNILEVER).

In 1990, Shell pushed past EXXON to become the world's largest oil company. Its strategy seems to be one of stockpiling — both oil under the 400 million acres that it owns, and several billion dollars in cash. For the 1990s the company (understandably) sees the environmental challenge as one of the most important that it faces.

## SALOMON BROTHERS

The brokerage firm that most epitomized the brash "anything goes" culture of Wall Street in the 1980s. It increased its staff by 40% in 1986 alone and was the subject of one of the funniest books ever written about the finance industry, Michael Lewis's *Liar's Poker*.

The firm finally met its nemesis in 1990, when it was found to have fiddled a U.S. treasury-bond auction. The firm's **CHAIRMAN** and its **PRESIDENT** (Michael Lewis's father-in-law) resigned immediately, and its biggest single shareholder (Warren Buffett) became chairman. It took full-page advertisements in the world's press to announce how penitent it was, but it was shunned by all sorts of blue-chip customers, including the World Bank.

Morale sank low as free-wheeling staff members were told that the firm's new code of behavior forbade them to do anything that they would be ashamed for their wives and children to read in the headlines of their local newspaper.

## SAS

Scandinavian Airline Systems, owned by a complicated mix of public- and private-sector interests in Sweden, Norway, and Denmark, very successfully carved a niche for itself as the businessperson's choice of airline in the 1980s. Its chairman, Jan Carlzon, became a cult figure with a best-selling book and a reputation for inspiring thousands at informal staff meetings in aircraft hangars.

But even Carlzon could not steer the airline through the clouds of the Gulf War and subsequent recession.

SAS had losses in two successive years and set out to ensure its survival with a series of strategic alliances with such airlines as Swissair and Austrian Airlines. It also bought a quarter of a small U.K. airline, British Midland.

## SATISFICING

A concept that undermines the classical economists' view that human behavior is determined by a search for what is best among a number of alternatives. Satisficing is the choosing of an option (not necessarily "the best") that reaches a minimum acceptable level. It recognizes that in many instances where they have to make decisions, human beings are unable to consider all the options available. They therefore go for the one they come across that best meets their minimum standards. They are "satisficers," not "maximizers."

This has obvious applications for corporate behavior and STRATEGY. Managers are also often satisficers, plumping for targets and achievements that are acceptable to their firm and to their industry. If they make a determined attempt to maximize their performance, they may find that they can soar way above the industry norms.

## SCENARIO PLANNING

The business of drawing up the background "noise" against which an individual company's strategy is to be played out. Everything in the future is uncertain; but for the purposes of formulating STRATEGY, certain macroeconomic, social, and scientific assumptions have to be made. Rather than rely on a single set of assumptions, scenario planning evaluates the impact of a number of different sets of assumptions, often categorized as "best case" and "worst case." This process enables managers to think more realistically about their response to an uncertain future. Big companies have spent much effort in creating computer-based systems that can generate different scenarios on the basis of different assumptions. Against these different backgrounds, different strategies can be painted.

Scenario planning was developed by the oil company **ROYAL DUTCH/SHELL** at a time when the military strategic model was being discredited. Creating a single plan to be followed with military precision simply did not work in the real business world.

### SCHLUMBERGER

Founded in Paris by two Alsatian brothers, headquartered in New York, and registered in the Netherlands Antilles, this polyglot company is an outstanding leader in the niche business of "wireline logging," a way of taking X-rays of possible oil and gas wells. It maintains its competitive edge (and profits of over $500 million) by living up to its reputation for producing state-of-the-art equipment for the very demanding oil industry.

### SCORCHED-EARTH DEFENSE

A defense against **TAKEOVER** that involves destroying (or selling) large parts of the business, or at least ensuring that they will be destroyed should they be taken over. A rather drastic defense, it also involves an awkward irony: What to do if it succeeds and the suitor is deterred? How do you make grass grow again on scorched earth? (See also **CROWN JEWELS, PAC-MAN DEFENSE, POISON PILL,** and **SHARK REPELLANT**)

### SEGMENTATION

The process of dividing a market into its different segments. This enables a product to be more carefully tailored for that subset of the market to which it is most likely to appeal. For example, take shampoos: there are shampoos for thin hair, for dry hair, for those with dandruff, for those who wash their hair every day, and so on.

There are many different criteria by which to segment a market. The existence or absence of dandruff is not one of the more common. For large-ticket items there is almost always a group of buyers that values premium features such as convenience, availability of service, and durability. These buyers form the luxury segment present in many markets.

Segmentation enables a firm to determine where the strongest competition lies within its market and to find out where (or whether) there is an as-yet untouched NICHE on which it can most profitably concentrate its efforts.

Segmentation's drawbacks lie in its inability to realize fully ECONOMIES OF SCALE and in the danger of a segment disappearing as buyers' needs change over time.

### SELF-MANAGED TEAMS

These groups of empowered employees do not have managers, although former management personnel may act as coaches, advisers, or facilitators. Self-managed teams take responsibility for establishing work rules, setting schedules, organizing production, and even evaluating performance. To work effectively, self-managed teams need to be given access to information normally held by management and must have the freedom to make their own mistakes. The result is increased QUAL-ITY, PRODUCTIVITY, and customer satisfaction.

### SENSITIVITY ANALYSIS

"What-if" questions that determine how sensitive a BUSINESS PLAN or budget is to changes in its underlying assumptions. Every plan has to assume certain things about the general macroeconomic background and about the microeconomic behavior of the firm. Sensitivity analysis attempts to answer this question: What happens to our planned outcome if our assumptions are $x\%$ adrift? It enables the analyst to determine which assumptions have a critical impact on the bottom line. At that point, the organization can take steps to improve the reliability of these assumptions or to minimize their impact.

The increasing availability of cheap computing power has enabled sensitivity analysis to be carried out rapidly and cost effectively. The problem then becomes one of choice. If a manager knows the ultimate outcome of a thousand different sets of possibilities, it does not necessarily make decision making any easier.

### SEVEN SS

A framework for thinking about the structure of organizations, first developed by the management consulting firm MCKINSEY and then popularized in a number of books written by ex-McKinsey consultants. One example: *The Art of Japanese Management* by Richard Pascale.

The 7-S framework maintains that there are seven interrelated factors that determine the effectiveness of an organization. The classical pair — structure and

STRATEGY — plus five others that all happen to begin with the letter S:

1. **Structure** — how the firm is organized.

2. **Strategy** — the route an organization decides to follow in order to achieve its goals.

3. **Systems** — the formal and informal procedures that govern everyday activity.

4. **Skill** — the unique competencies of the organization.

5. **Style** — how the management presents itself to other employees, and how the entire workforce presents itself to the outside world.

6. **Superordinate goals** — the fundamental philosophy underlying an organization. This was subsequently retitled "Shared values in search of EXCELLENCE."

7. **Staff** — the quality of the firm's human resources.

In bringing about change within an organization, proponents of the 7-S theory maintain that equal attention must be given to each of the seven Ss. No one is more important than another. The first four Ss are sometimes called the hard Ss and receive most of management's attention. The three soft Ss are more difficult to change, but just as crucial.

### SHAREHOLDER WEALTH

The total market value of the firm; that is, the stock price multiplied by the total number of shares outstanding.

Maximizing shareholder wealth is generally the objective of every firm. An undervalued firm becomes a likely target for TAKEOVER: in the 1980s, when takeovers occurred frequently, systematic management of shareholder wealth became a strategic objective, as top management was advised to "manage the company like a raider," presumably to defend against a hostile takeover attempt. Companies pursuing this defense strategy carefully managed the physical assets of the business, cash flow from ongoing operations, and investors' expectations of additional growth from internal development.

As a STRATEGY, maximizing shareholder wealth has been criticized because it forces companies to focus narrowly on its short-term financial results and not its fundamental operating competencies over the long term.

### SHARK REPELLANT

A smell put out by a company to deter potential suitors. For example, a leaked announcement about a "secret" contract to pay millions to existing managers should the company be taken over. (See also CROWN JEWELS, PAC-MAN DEFENSE, POISON PILL, and SCORCHED-EARTH DEFENSE)

### SLEEPING BEAUTY

A company that has not yet been spotted as the great takeover target that it is (because of some hidden asset — a valuable patent, perhaps, or a particularly desirable piece of property). A sleeping beauty can also be a product or service whose time has not quite come.

### SMALL FIRMS

With his famous book, *Small is Beautiful* (the title was his publisher's idea), E. F. Schumacher may not have convinced everybody of his thesis; but he and others have convinced everybody that small is special, and in need of special treatment. Small companies account for a disproportionately high proportion of the INNOVATION in companies everywhere.

Few, if any, firms are born big. They start small, and some grow. Many governments believe that these firms, especially when they are in significant infant and high-tech industries, need protection, in particular from foreign competition, until they reach a sustainable size. Schumacher maintained that "organizations should imitate nature, which doesn't allow a single cell to become too large."

### SOCIAL RESPONSIBILITY

The idea — gaining ever-greater currency, particularly among Japanese companies — that a company has a duty toward the community in which it operates, a duty that goes beyond the passive one of not actually causing harm to that community (or its environment).

A company's social responsibility extends to giving positive support to the community — through charities, or sponsorship, and so forth. This responsibility arises, if for nothing else, as a result of the immeasurable benefit that the company gains from the fact that the community and its infrastructure is there for it to use.

### SONY

The most famous Japanese company and inventor of the Walkman, a word now found in the venerable *Oxford English Dictionary*. Headed for many years by the most famous Japanese businessman outside Japan, Akio Morita. Although it seems venerable, the company was founded in 1946 and changed its name to Sony as recently as 1958.

Like its great rival MATSUSHITA, Sony has tried to

avoid overdependence on its "hard" audio and video products, and has bought into American software firms; it paid $2 billion for the CBS record company in 1987, and $3.4 billion for the Columbia movie company in 1989.

Sony has also moved further than any other Japanese company in its efforts to become truly international, and the company is committed to going even further: "Having gained recognition as one of Japan's most international companies by manufacturing in the markets where its products are sold, Sony is expanding its other corporate functions, such as management and R&D, on a global basis." Much of its pioneering research into HDTV (high-definition television, the next great consumer durable) has been done in the United States.

---

*Japan's competitiveness has been achieved by keeping margins and prices low over a long time in a constant search for volume to provide cash flow. This has meant skimping other stakeholders in favor of the customer.*

*Japan must fashion a new corporate attitude, rebalancing stakeholder interests, and going some way to meet the West.*

Akio Morita, Sony, 1992

---

## SPAN OF CONTROL

The number of people that any one manager can cope with under his or her direct control. There are many different theories about what is the ideal number: it certainly varies from individual to individual, and it certainly has a significant bearing on the structure of organizations. The most popular candidate is probably seven.

### SPIN-OFF

A new company created to pursue an idea that the parent is not willing to undertake. Often very worthwhile businesses are spun off because they do not fit with what the company considers its core businesses.

There have been many examples in soft industries — such as publishing and computer software — where the startup costs are not enormous. Some companies, however, arrange their own spin-offs. They encourage employees to pursue their ideas and take a minority stake in the enterprise just in case it proves to be a big success. Almost invariably they are able to increase their minority stake when the spin-off runs up against a need for new capital.

### STAKEHOLDER

Interest groups to which the corporation is accountable. Stockholders and owners are not the only ones whose expectations must be met; others include employees, creditors, suppliers, the community, and government agencies. Each group has different, often conflicting, needs that affect the corporation's ability to execute a STRATEGY.

### STANDARDIZATION

Standardization is an intrinsic element of a global STRATEGY as companies seek opportunities for GLOBAL

ECONOMIES OF SCALE. Products such as electronics can be standardized globally. Others — chocolate, for example — remain subject to local preference.

Companies have to pay close attention to rules devised by international bodies on the standardization of products and processes. This can be costly. The benefit comes because many government organizations buy only products that accord with international standards. And in some cases it is illegal to sell nonstandardized products.

Government demands for standardization have sometimes been thinly disguised forms of protectionism. The Japanese are past masters at this, once devising standards for skis and ski equipment based on the unique nature and dangers of Japanese snow. Needless to say, no American or European manufacturers' products came up to those standards.

### STATISTICAL TESTING

This has had a central role in the recent corporate obsession with QUALITY. Statistics — that part of mathematics concerned with the collection, organization, and analysis of data — were deeply embedded in the original ideas of W. Edwards Deming about quality, and in Japanese companies' applications of them.

Quality control consists of taking a sample periodically from a product's output and measuring certain aspects of it. These readings are then plotted on a quality control chart that has lines on it (called control limits) representing the acceptable limits of each measure. (See also PROBABILITY)

### STRATEGIC ALLIANCE

See ALLIANCE

## Strategic Business Unit (SBU)

The smallest unit within a corporation that can independently put into effect a **STRATEGY**. SBUs (sometimes known as strategy centers) are capable of being divested and run as stand-alone businesses. As such, the SBU has identifiable competitors, competes in an external market, and includes relevant functional areas.

SBUs often bundle together businesses that straddle traditional organizational lines. But they may simply consist of a whole product line. **GENERAL ELECTRIC** pioneered the SBU as the basis for strategic planning. The SBU once occupied center stage as the basis for strategy development. It is being replaced by concepts such as **BUSINESS PROCESS** and **CORE COMPETENCE.**

### Strategic fit

The degree of matching between a company's strategy and its resources — capital, people, and equipment.

### Strategic group

Those firms within an industry that are pursuing similar strategies are said to constitute a strategic group. Within an industry there will often be some firms aiming to be the **COST LEADER** while others are targeting a small market niche. By dividing firms into their different strategic groups it is possible to analyze an industry and find useful pointers as to which strategy might be successful in that industry in the future.

### Strategic intent

A term introduced by Gary Hamel and C. K. Prahalad in an article of the same name published in the *Harvard Business Review* in 1990. It refers to those overwhelming corporate goals designed to inspire a company and its employees over a period of at least a decade. Examples include Coca-Cola's aim to put Coke within "arm's reach of every consumer in the world."

---

*We know that without leaders who "walk the talk," all our plans, promises and dreams for the future are just that — talk.*

General Electric

---

### STRATEGIC PLANNING

A process for drawing up a company's strategic map, the route whereby it will provide what products to what customers, where, and at what price.

The person who virtually invented strategic planning was Igor Ansoff, an engineer who worked for Lockheed as a long-term planner. A fellow management guru said of Ansoff's book, *Corporate Strategy*, that it is "the most elaborate model of strategic planning in the literature." The book, in Ansoff's words, sought "to develop a practical method for strategic decision-making within a business firm." Some found it so detailed and full of checklists that it could be used to program a computer to draw up a corporate strategy.

At one point strategic planning existed as a separate function in many large corporations. This led to the criticism that the strategic plan was imposed from on high and led to half-hearted implementation. Now divisions are usually responsible for their own strategic plans.

## STRATEGY

A general policy for achieving a number of specified objectives. As Michael Porter once put it, "The word global, like the word strategy, has become overused and perhaps misunderstood."

The word came originally from a Greek word meaning generalship, and until recently it had a very specific military meaning: the art of planning and conducting war.

---

*Planning is everything. The plan is nothing.*

General Dwight D. Eisenhower

---

## SUBSTITUTION

The use of one product to perform the functions of another. A consumer could substitute a VCR and rented videotapes for a subscription to Home Box Office, a premium cable TV channel. In developing competitive strategy it is important to assess the potential impact of substitute products. They influence demand for the products, their price, and profitability. Substitute products create a whole new set of competitors.

## SUCCESSION PLANNING

A formal procedure for determining who is to follow the boss. With a touch of irony, this is considered by some to be the prime responsibility of a CHIEF EXECUTIVE OFFICER: to identify and groom a successor. The task differs according to whether the company is a public company or a private (family-controlled) business. The heads of family-controlled companies almost always leave their business in the hands of someone who shares their genes — or who married someone who shares their genes.

In public companies there are a number of ways of choosing a successor. One survey found that out of a sample of 400 big American companies, nearly three-quarters had a succession plan — and two out of every three of those with a plan had developed it at board level.

Some companies set succession up as a horse race — which tends to produce tough no-nonsense bosses like Jack Welch at **GENERAL ELECTRIC**, a man who won a succession race against four other horses, and John Reed at **CITICORP**, who won against two other horses.

A major issue for succession in a public company is whether to pick from inside the company or to look outside. Insiders tend to reinforce the direction that the company is already following; the selection of an outsider tends to demoralize insiders who aspired to the top job. And on occasion it persuades other top managers to depart. (But then the internal horse race usually sends some of the losing horses packing too.)

### Sunrise industry

Popular expression for **EMERGENT INDUSTRY**.

### Sunset industry

Popular expression for **DECLINING INDUSTRY**. (See also **INDUSTRIAL LIFE CYCLE**)

### Sweat

As in "make the assets sweat," "sweat shop," and "sweat equity" — making things more productive in a decidedly unrelaxed way.

## SWOT

A mnemonic for four key questions that any company needs to think about:

- **Strengths.** What are the company's strengths compared with those of its competitors?
- **Weaknesses.** What are its weaknesses, compared with those of its competitors?
- **Opportunities.** What are the main opportunities for the company in its surrounding environment?
- **Threats.** What are the main threats to it in its surrounding environment?

There are some who prefer to call it TOWS rather than SWOT — thereby placing emphasis on the questions about corporate environment rather than on the questions about the company itself. (See also COMPETITIVE ADVANTAGE)

### SYNERGY

When the combined effect of putting two things together exceeds the sum of the two things — that is, making $2 + 2 = 5$. In the 1970s, synergy was a strategic buzzword, the holy grail sought by many companies in pursuit of DIVERSIFICATION. For example, food manufacturers went into paper and packaging on the grounds that there was synergy to be gained from using the packaging to ship the fruit; airlines bought hotels to gain synergy from putting their passengers into their beds.

In the late 1980s, synergy went out of fashion. People such as Michael Porter introduced other ways of thinking about adding value when putting businesses and bits of businesses together (see VALUE CHAIN). Synergy, however, can still be a useful concept if it is not assumed that it somehow works automatically on all occasions.

## Takeover

When one company obtains a majority of the shares in another. This can be achieved in two ways:

- As a "friendly" takeover, in which the company being taken over courts it.
- As a "hostile" takeover, in which the company being taken over fights to prevent the "predator" from obtaining a majority of its shares.

A company can take many different types of defense if it becomes the subject of a hostile takeover (see **CROWN JEWELS, PAC-MAN DEFENSE, POISON PILL, SCORCHED-EARTH DEFENSE,** and **SHARK REPELLANT**). One way in which hostile predators steal a march on those they wish to take over is by means of a **DAWN RAID**.

In Anglo-Saxon economies takeovers are fought as games in which both sides must follow "fair" rules. The guiding principles are that shareholders' interests come uppermost and that all shareholders be treated equally.

In continental Europe and Japan neither of these principles is widely respected. Different voting rights attaching to different categories of shares ensure that shareholders are never equal, least of all at the time of a potential takeover. And the general shareholder's interest is often subsumed under that of a ruling coterie, family, or financial institution.

*I always say to executives that they ought to go and see King Lear, because they'll be out*

*there too one day, wandering on the heath*
*without a company car.*

Charles Handy

---

### TARGET

A company that has been identified as being a desirable candidate for a TAKEOVER.

### TASK FORCE

A TEAM brought together from different parts of an organization in order to carry out a particular task. This may be short term (for example, for CRISIS MANAGEMENT), or it may be longer term, involving the development of a new product, for example, from the drawing board to the shop window. Once its task is completed, a task force is disbanded.

### TEAM

Teams are used when a task requires a combination of multiple skills, experience, and judgments. The use of teams is increasing because they are more flexible than larger organizational groupings. They can be quickly assembled, displayed, refocused, and disbanded (see also SELF-MANAGED TEAMS).

McKinsey consultants Jon Katzenbach and Douglas Smith list six rules for team leaders:

1. Keep the purpose, goals, and approach relevant and meaningful.

2. Build commitment and confidence through constructive reinforcement, not intimidation.

3. Strengthen the mix and level of skills; make sure

the team has all the skills it needs to accomplish its goals.

4. Manage relationships with outsiders and remove obstacles.

5. Create opportunities for others; share the credit.

6. Do real work. When "dirty work" is required, the team leader should be the first to step forward.

## 3M

A manufacturer of not very glamorous products (like Scotch Tape and Post-it notes) that invariably appears on lists of the best-managed companies in America. Born in the early years of this century as the Minnesota Mining & Manufacturing Company, it soon dropped the Mining to concentrate full time on the Manufacturing. It changed its name to 3M (one of the most difficult to know where to file), despite the fact that there are now only two Ms that are relevant — the company's headquarters are still in St. Paul, Minnesota.

In their book *In Search of Excellence*, Tom Peters and Robert Waterman held up 3M as a paragon of EXCELLENCE.

> *Its [3M's] trick has been to understand value-added differentiation and perpetual market creation long before such action became necessary. Every unit of the corporation, whether it serves mature markets or exotic new ones, is charged with continual reinvention. And the firm's minimum acceptable profit margins per unit are astronomical — only attainable with truly superior products and service.*

The company makes some 60,000 different products and aims to ensure that at least 25% of its turnover comes from products that have been in existence for less than five years.

---

*On top of a small bedrock of certainty swirls an almost random and often frantic search for solutions to new problems. Some might see that as the best way to bring up children. It may also be the best way to bring up managers.*

*EuroBusiness* on 3M

---

### TIME-BASED COMPETITION

In their book *Competing Against Time*, BCGers George Stalk, Jr., and Thomas Hout showed readers a powerful new source of competitive advantage — reducing time in production, new product development and introduction, and sales and distribution. Practiced most successfully in Japan, time-based competitors reorganized factories, distribution systems, and information as well as other support systems to reduce delays and in so doing improved **PRODUCTIVITY, QUALITY**, and got closer to their customers. Manufacturing processes were improved by reducing the length of production runs, reorganizing components of the manufacturing process, and simplifying scheduling procedures. Labor costs are reduced when the work is simplified, productivity improves, less management time is required, and inventory carrying costs are reduced as manufacturing time shortens. In addition, as the lag between order and delivery shortens, customer satisfaction improves.

The concept has been applied with even more devastating (to competitors) results to product innovation. By applying many of the same principles to product development, time-based Japanese competitors have reduced development time to months rather than the years typical of Western competitors.

### Toshiba

The Japanese electronics firm that developed the market for portable computers with its user-friendly "Tosh." It has a wide network of joint ventures — the most significant of which is one with IBM to produce large color liquid-crystal display (LCD) units, which Toshiba believes are "the wave of the future in computer hardware."

### Total Quality Management (TQM)

A "movement" that swept across America in the 1980s like a corporate religion. At best somewhat fuzzy, it usually referred to those things required of companies to enable them to exceed their customers' expectations. Such things included quality circles, quality control, and "total customer satisfaction" with the quality of the product and of the service element in the product. By the end of the 1980s the movement had swept into Europe, supported strongly by firms such as **VOLVO** and **PHILIPS** that were feeling most threatened by Japanese competition. (See **QUALITY MANAGEMENT**)

### Toyota

The biggest and most conservative Japanese car maker. One of the largest companies in the world in terms of turnover, it is still managed in some ways like the family firm that it once was. In 1992, the company's **CHAIR-MAN**, Eiji Toyoda [sic], retired and was replaced by his nephew Shoichiro Toyoda, who moved up from the job of **PRESIDENT** (in Toyota, as in most Japanese companies, this is equivalent to **CHIEF EXECUTIVE OFFICER**). Shoichiro Toyoda was replaced as president by his younger brother Tatsuro Toyoda.

The founding Toyoda family insisted that this was the last Toyoda to get the top job. There are no other family members in top management posts. It is nevertheless remarkable that a company that has made annual profits of over $4 billion, and is quoted on several of the world's major bourses, should still be so dominated by its founding family.

Through a strategy of **CONTINUOUS IMPROVEMENT** (*kaizen*), Toyota excels in **QUALITY**, **PRODUCTIVITY**, and efficiency. Toyota's luxury sedan, the Lexus, is built with one-sixth of the labor needed to manufacture a Mercedes.

Toyota originated **JUST-IN-TIME** production. While other automakers use JIT mainly for the delivery of parts to the assembly line, Toyota's entire production process is built around the concept. Toyota dealers in Japan use on-line computers to order cars directly from the factory; the customer can get a built-to-order car in a week to 10 days. Since there are virtually no inventories and no unsold cars sitting on the dealers' lots, there are substantial cost savings. Equally important, the factory can balance production as demand shifts.

*Demand does not happen by itself.*

Shoichiro Toyoda

## TRADE FAIR

The gathering together of a host of producers (from the same industry) under one roof, where they show off their wares to one another and to potential customers.

Trade fairs have become a bit like Hollywood movies — they fall into two categories:

1. Those that everybody must attend, to see and be seen at. If this means lining up around the block during a rainstorm, so be it.

2. Those that nobody wants to bother with, but that try so desperately hard to attract your attendance that you send a junior trainee who needs a trip out of the office.

The former include such heavyweights as the Frankfurt Book Fair and a host of industrial engineering fairs held in Germany. They also include particularly glamorous trade fairs like the Geneva Motor Show and the Cannes Film Festival. Some of the most successful trade fairs are for unlikely products such as gift items.

The strategic issues to focus on:

- How to get the best location at the "essential" fairs.
- Which second-ranking fairs to attend, and in what strength. This should be determined largely by whether the local market (in the country where the fair is located), is, or is likely to be, interesting. But never forget that much good business has been done as a result of chance meetings at second-rate fairs.

## TRADE-OFF

Mutually exclusive alternatives. Business, like life, is full of such choices — growth or market share? Make or buy? When choosing between alternatives it is helpful to list the pluses and minuses of each option.

## TRANSACTION COST

The cost involved in carrying out a transaction. It is most apparent with cases like the buying and selling of securities, foreign exchange, or antiques at auction. Anybody selling these things does not get the full price for them because an agent (the broker or auctioneer) has to be paid in order to sell them at all. This is a transaction cost. More widespread are the transaction costs involved in buying or selling a property: the estate agent's commission, the lawyer's fees, and the government's tax or duty.

There are also some rather less obvious transaction costs that go unaccounted for when calculating whether a deal is worth doing: these include the time spent finding out information on a potential new customer's creditworthiness — or about an alternative supplier's reliability and delivery times. These costs may eliminate much of any benefit that can be gained from the transaction.

## TRANSFER PRICING

The vexing question of what price a company should charge for goods and services that are transferred internally from one part of the company to another: particularly pertinent when the transfer takes place across international borders. If it is accepted that full and accurate costing is an essential prerequisite to drawing up successful strategies, then so are decisions on transfer pricing. Such decisions also have to balance the need to benefit from the company's overall structure (by minimizing tax payments, for example) with the need not to discourage managers of individual STRATEGIC BUSINESS UNITS (SBUs) by loading them with costs that are not fairly theirs.

*Our preferred method for determining the transfer prices is to take the market price; where there is no market price, the two managements concerned engage in arms' length negotiations. Where required, the method employed is discussed and agreed with the government authorities of the countries concerned.*

Unilever

## TREND ANALYSIS

The pervasive business practice of looking at charts of behavior in the past (of sales, profits, and so on), and from them analyzing trends into the future. This is useful, but within carefully defined limits — limits that exist because the future is never ever a repeat of the past, and because trend analysis discourages management from thinking laterally — that is, freed from the chains of its own past experience. (See also REGRESSION ANALYSIS)

## TURNAROUND TIME

The amount of time that it takes to get a particular job done from the moment it is begun to the moment it is finished. It can apply to something as simple as the unloading of a truck, or as complicated as the manufacture of a high-fashion garment — from the time it is ordered to the time that it is delivered to the buyer's premises.

## Unilever

Europe's answer to (and great rival of) the American consumer-products group **PROCTER & GAMBLE**. Unilever consists of two companies — one Dutch and one British. Each has the same board of directors, and a three-person chief executive (known as the Special Committee). They are linked by agreements that effectively make them one unit, but with dual nationality.

Unilever's brands include Brooke Bond, Walls, Persil, and Elizabeth Arden. In the 1980s, it retrenched to its four core businesses: detergents, food, agribusiness, and cosmetics. It sold about 100 companies and bought about 120. Now it aims "to be the foremost company in meeting the daily needs of consumers across the world in its chosen markets." Like Procter & Gamble, it lays great emphasis on **INNOVATION**: "Innovation through science and technology lies at the core of competitive advantage in Unilever's markets."

## Value-added

The difference between the selling price of a product and the cost of purchased inputs. The objective of all capitalist business activity is to earn a profit by adding value. A value-added chain describes the sequence of activities through which value is added as a product changes from raw material to finished product and is delivered to an end-user. Perhaps because they track the flow of goods, like rivers, value chains begin upstream and move **DOWNSTREAM** from raw material to end-user.

A business activity may not span an entire value chain. If it does, this business is referred to as fully integrated. The decision about which steps or links of the chain to include is a strategic one. When a manufacturer opens a factory outlet, it is moving downstream to capture value-added at the retail stage.

## Value chain

Michael Porter introduced this concept in his 1985 book, *Competitive Advantage: Creating and Sustaining Superior Performance.* An adaptation of the **VALUE-ADDED** chain, the value chain includes five primary or direct activities (inbound logistics, operations, outbound logistics, marketing/sales, and service) and four support or indirect activities (firm infrastructure, **HUMAN RESOURCE MANAGEMENT**, technology development, and procurement). The direct activities occur in sequence, the indirect support all of the direct activities. Value chains vary by industry and by firm. Competitive advantage is gained by exploiting or creating linkages between elements of the chain to achieve **DIFFERENTIATION** or reduced costs.

## VENTURE CAPITAL

Considered by many to be the core of the entrepreneurial process, venture capital has played a central role in the development of important new industries, including personal computers, cellular communications, microcomputer software, and biotechnology.

Venture capital is essential to cash-hungry startup businesses, which typically experience negative cash flows for seven or more years. Traditional lenders — banks and institutional investors — cannot assume the risk associated with these investments. Venture capitalists provide these funds and expect their reward in the form of capital gains when the young firm eventually goes public. Venture capital firms try to add value by identifying and evaluating business opportunities (including management), supplying entry or growth strategy, coaching, providing technical and management assistance, and attracting additional capital, directors, and other key resources.

## VERTICAL INTEGRATION

An integrated firm participates in more than one contiguous stage of the value-added chain. If a firm adds upstream activities, it "backward integrates." If it adds downstream activities, it "forward integrates." The key strategic TRADE-OFF involved is that the integrated firm usually has lower costs but substantially less flexibility than its nonintegrated competitor.

## VIRGIN

The MAVERICK British airline that took on the transatlantic airline OLIGOPOLY after the failure of Laker Airways to crack the powerful European and American CARTEL. Virgin attempted to differentiate its service and, unburdened with the overheads of running unprofitable routes (it flew only on prime routes like London–Miami and London–Tokyo), caused a stir in the industry.

It also brought home the fact that airlines are less in the business of transporting passengers, and more in the business of elbowing rivals out of their most valuable (and limited) resource — landing and take-off "slots" at the world's favorite airports (e.g., Heathrow, Kennedy, and Narita).

## VISION

A necessary part of any STRATEGY — an irrational barrier-leaping ambition for a company. First find your vision, then devise a strategy to achieve it. (See also MISSION STATEMENT)

---

*In business, as in life, we all need a purpose beyond ourselves to feel useful, worthwhile and good about ourselves.*

Charles Handy

---

## VOLVO

The Swedish car company that formed a pioneering alliance with France's Renault in 1990 in what could be a forerunner of other alliances in the mature European motor industry. The two firms agreed to pool their R&D, design, component manufacture, and procurement, and swapped shares in their respective car and truck divisions.

Volvo's executive **CHAIRMAN** Pehr Gyllenhammar has been a leading light in the total quality movement in Europe, and much emphasis has been laid on the quality aspects of the venture with Renault. Volvo is also famous for its efforts at job enrichment and for its decentralized decision making. (It has an HQ staff of only 100.) For all its progressive management, however, the company could not avoid a very lean patch in the early 1990s.

## WAL-MART

Under the leadership of founder Sam Walton, Wal-Mart has become the number-one retailer in the United States. Annual growth is about 25%, compared to an industry average of 4%; the company's operating and selling expenses are a lean 15% of sales, compared to 28% for the moribund Sears, Roebuck and Co.

From modest beginnings in Bentonville, Arkansas, the company has expanded aggressively since going public in 1970. The company's original STRATEGY was to put large discount stores in small towns (primarily in the South) that had been ignored by competitors such as K mart. Wal-Mart's winning COMPETITIVE ADVANTAGE has been built on value, QUALITY, and service.

Wal-Mart has led the retail industry in many innovative practices while preaching old-fashioned values and sustaining a strong CORPORATE CULTURE (complete with a company cheer). Sites for new stores are scouted from the air. Hourly employees (called "associates") are offered stock through a payroll deduction plan. Wal-Mart executives spend most of their time visiting stores and customers, and meet every Saturday at 7 A.M. to share information and solve problems. Information on an individual store's sales, profits, purchases, and markdowns is shared with all employees.

Wal-Mart is revolutionizing the structure of the retail industry through its aggressive use of information technology and CHANNEL PARTNERSHIPS. The company has established a close relationship with PROCTER & GAMBLE, which has dedicated a 70-person team to work with Wal-Mart. The two companies share an information system that has enabled P&G to take over Wal-Mart's purchasing function. P&G assembles orders and replenishes inventory in Wal-Mart's distribution centers based on daily point-of-sale data from Wal-Mart stores. There are no invoices; payment is triggered automatically when the product is received.

---

*. . . a lot of bureaucracy is really the product of some empire builder's ego. Some folks have a tendency to build up big staffs around them to emphasize their own importance, and we don't need any of that at Wal-Mart. If you're not serving the customer, or supporting the folks who do, we don't need you.*

Sam Walton in *Sam Walton: Made in America*

---

### WHITE KNIGHT

A firm that comes to the rescue of a company in the throes of an unwelcome TAKEOVER.

### WINDOW DRESSING

The universal practice of making published accounts look as attractive as they can possibly (i.e., legally) be. The expression implies that there is something not quite nice about a company that hides its darker side from public view.

But many companies would not be in business if they did not indulge in this regular fantasy. Should Christian

Dior reveal all the sweated labor and heartache behind its every shimmering creation? Why value an asset at $x when it can justifiably be valued at $2x?

The real danger from window dressing is not that it will fool its audience (although that might matter, depending on the circumstances); it is that it will fool its authors: the company's managers. Many companies have hit the rocks because top managers took their (fantastical) accounts too literally.

### WINDOW OF OPPORTUNITY

A STRATEGY's effectiveness can depend entirely on timing — there are right times and wrong times to take certain steps. New products are launched only at certain seasons (not the week before Christmas, for example); and there are good and bad times for going to the stock market with a new issue. Miss a window of opportunity and, at best, you have to wait a while.

## ZERO-BASE BUDGETING

An important way of escaping from the bind of beginning all annual budgeting on the basis of last year's figures and adding a fixed percentage to them all. Zero-base budgeting involves justifying every budget item afresh every year. While this can strip away some unnecessary costs that have been blindly taken for granted, it can take a lot of extra time, time that in many cases is not justified by the saving. It is useful as a method that managers are aware *might* be employed should they be too slaphappy with more traditional budgeting methods.